YOU ARE MEANT TO BE LOVED

Jesus, The Ultimate Superhero

Louresta Dodson-Lankard

BALBOA.PRESS

A DIVISION OF HAY HOUSE

Balboa Press books may be ordered through booksellers or by contacting:

Balboa Press
A Division of Hay House
1663 Liberty Drive
Bloomington, IN 47403
www.balboapress.com
844-682-1282

Because of the dynamic nature of the Internet, any web addresses or links contained in this book may have changed since publication and may no longer be valid. The views expressed in this work are solely those of the author and do not necessarily reflect the views of the publisher, and the publisher hereby disclaims any responsibility for them.

The author of this book does not dispense medical advice or prescribe the use of any technique as a form of treatment for physical, emotional, or medical problems without the advice of a physician, either directly or indirectly. The intent of the author is only to offer information of a general nature to help you in your quest for emotional and spiritual well-being. In the event you use any of the information in this book for yourself, which is your constitutional right, the author and the publisher assume no responsibility for your actions.

Any people depicted in stock imagery provided by Getty Images are models, and such images are being used for illustrative purposes only. Certain stock imagery © Getty Images.

Scripture quotations marked KJV are taken from the King James Version.

Scripture quotations marked NKJV are taken from the New King James Version. Copyright © 1982 by Thomas Nelson, Inc. Used by permission. All rights reserved.

Scripture quotations marked NIV are taken from the Holy Bible, New International Version®. NIV®. Copyright © 1973, 1978, 1984 by International Bible Society. Used by permission of Zondervan. All rights reserved. [Biblica]

Scripture quotations marked NASB are taken from the New American Standard Bible®, Copyright © 1960, 1962, 1963, 1968, 1971, 1972, 1973, 1975, 1977, 1995 by The Lockman Foundation. Used by permission.

Scripture quotations marked HCSB are from the Holman Christian Standard Bible®. HCSB®. Copyright ©1999, 2000, 2002, 2003 by Holman Bible Publishers. Used by permission. Holman Christian Standard Bible®, Holman CSB®, and HCSB® are federally registered trademarks of Holman Bible Publishers

Print information available on the last page.

ISBN: 978-1-9822-6487-1 (sc)
ISBN: 978-1-9822-6489-5 (hc)
ISBN: 978-1-9822-6488-8 (e)

Library of Congress Control Number: 2021904062

Balboa Press rev. date: 02/25/2021

Freedom is not a gift bestowed upon us by other men, but a right that belongs to us by the laws of God and nature.

—John Webbe

I HAVE DIED THREE TIMES AND THEY KEEP SENDING ME BACK HERE!

If you have picked up this book out of curiosity, it is not a coincidence; you have been led to remember and to wake up. You may share some or most of my experiences. No matter what others think, you are not crazy; you're just trying to survive in a crazy, fallen, and broken world. What you might not know is that we live in a very magical and user-friendly universe, if you truly seek the truth as God would have you understand it. Whatever you think or whatever your focus is, whatever you are feeling is what you attract. This feeling becomes believing, perceiving, achieving and your reality. Most references are taking from the king James version of the Bible.

TO THE KING OF THE SPIRITS!

Praises be to the God of Abraham, Isaac, and Jacob, the Holy One of Israel, Alpha and Omega, the Beginning and the End.

I give all praise and glory to Jehovah for his majestic and awesome goodness, mercy and grace. Blessed Be to the Holy Spirit for a mind to pray, a heart to seek ABBA's face, and the authority to bring my members into subjection and to share who we all are in God's eyes. I love you king

Yeshua, for your deep forgiveness, and your healing and abiding love for humanity.

I have had mystical experiences since I was a child. I have died three times and they keep sending me back to his realm. As a result, It was an ongoing battle to embrace and accept my gifts and abilities, which, at the time, I did not want nor understood. These included talking to animals, talking to and seeing spirits and dead people, astral projections, near-death experiences, walk-ins, premonitions, visions, aliens, and angelic encounters. (Some of it, while doing 20 years in the military traveling the world, and in the psyche wards towards the end of that learning season).

In the name of Yeshua by the power of his shed blood on the cross, the blood of the Lamb, the Holy Spirit, I Am That Am, has dictated this book to remind us all how very special we are and we are meant to be loved.

I consider myself a spiritual servant or light-worker. I volunteered before birth to help myself, the planet and our population to heal from the effects of fear, and I know I am here for a sacred purpose. I believe spiritual methods directed by God can heal any thing.

IF YOU HAVE PICKED UP THIS BOOK BY ACCIDENT, IT WAS NO ACCIDENT.

WARNING: This book is not written for average Religious Addicts; it's for those who are lost or conflicted because they have allowed traditions to get in the way of truth "or social-religious dogmas and interests. This is based upon my personal and professional experience with overcoming fear and hatred of this world. Through God (The LivingWord), Jesus (His Living Will), and The Holy Spirit (His Way, or God's Living Guide). If you are offended or angry by my words, talk to God about it. I am just taking dictation in my up close and personal journey, as I Asked, Seeked, and Knocked with Jehovah-God according to the formula and principles of Matthew 7:7-8. And God Answered! This is a guide to remind and reawaken you on your journey to your truth and happiness and to unlock your hidden powers so you can become everything God has created you to be.

In my humbled attempts to grasp, straddle understand and relay many concepts of frightening, confusing life scenarios, the only thing that made some sort of sense was the Bible. My hope is my journey inspires you and helps you grasp the beautiful truth that having God and the Holy Trinity in your life means: Being On the Winning

Team, Being Blessed Beyond Belief, Life Ever Lasting, Indescribable Joy, Peace and Miracles in-spite of current Biblical Tribulations. Initially, I was bombarded the spirit of with fear, I was too scared to ask God or others close in my life. I am insane?

MY SUPERHERO!

Our God is an awesome, He is my closest forever-friend, I tell him everything! He is my Super Hero and Creator of All Creations, and my dad! He told me I could call him "ABBA", and his son "YESUAH". I never heard of those names until I did some deep research and He felt I was ready to receive it. ABBA is the King of Spirits. He has many names. He already made and conquered Satan. Jehovah is a Waymaker, Promise Keeper, Miracle Worker, A Light In The Darkness. He is available 24/7 and meets us no matter where we are. When I was nine and seriously thinking about suicide, I went to God and wrote him these questions and left them on my headboard of my bed. This was his ultimate reply to me.

Who Am I?

"You are a letter from Me, written not with ink but with the Spirit of the living God. God sees the best in us.

It doesn't matter what we did. He only sees us for who we are. We are made in God's image. We have powers that we are unaware of. This book, through my life journey, is our collaborative effort is to get us to remember and reawaken the God-Light within, to unleash your personal truth and give you the courage to speak your truth, and to see who you really are. This book will challenge your current mind set, God wants to awaken us so we can walk confidently in the direction of your true self, your power, and your dreams. God said; "Lack is a universal lie devised by Satan. There is abundance, victory and peace for everyone who seeks his or her true self through the Jehovah-God. God gave me clarity and direction for myself and those who are seeking Gods truth based on insights and first hand experiences, I am experiencing how God is continually Blessing my life and those that I love.

What Am I?

I am a spiritual being, having a human experience. Earth is a kind of dimensional boot camp in the matrix of our minds. Overcoming fear, shame, and guilt is the goal. We volunteer for this journey. We are not only world travelers but interstellar, intergalactic travelers, carrying the light of God. Faith, hope, and love—positive thoughts for which God is Love, And Love is God.

Why Am I Here?

Let us remember that we are all connected and are working to bring about the new heaven and earth in this mind-over-matter experiment. We are seeking a greater understanding of how God's love is manifested through his love for man, which is the love for woman, an expression of the true meaning of God's Word through love. I would encourage you to be curious and to ask God to make his plan clear for you. Know that you are loved and cherished. As God's children, we were born perfect, are perfect, and are eternal, so expect miracles. You are a shining example of God's grace, and you will come out victorious.

What Is My Purpose?

I want to declare and decree victory, triumph, success, and defeat over darkness. I want to encourage and remind God's appointed, anointed, and empowered from a place of beingness. To bring about equality and balance to the universe, realizing all things affect one another in the tapestry of life and the universe. I believe, perceive, and achieve reawakening to your "Godlegitness"—yeah, I said Godlegitness—as you assume your divine birthright, living victoriously with purpose, passion, and praise.

DEDICATION

I declare grace and peace to you from God our Father and the Lord Jesus Christ. I give all honor to I AM that I AM, as I understand him. I declare and decree that all who seek the truth and believe that we are made in his image will be guided to seek and find truth through him as they journey the self with I AM that I AM. On this journey, I declare that by the power of the blood of Jesus Christ, all who seek the truth shall find it and understand God, as he would have us understand him. I declare that all who believe in I AM that I AM will be covered by the promises and blessings of the covenant of God's holy name. This is my declaration in the name of Jesus Christ and the power of his blood, amen, and amen.

From the fruit of their mouth a person's stomach is filled; with the harvest of their lips they are satisfied.
The tongue has the power of life and death,
and those who love it will eat its fruit.
—Proverbs 18:20–21 (NIV)

MISSION STATEMENT

I don't want to be right, I want to know the truth!
But seek first the kingdom of God and His
righteousness, and all these things shall be added to you.
—Matthew 6:33 (NKJV)

You will know the truth and the truth
shall set you free. (John 8:32)

I come from humble beginnings and have endured harsh life experiences that have made me stronger and wiser and have birthed awesome spiritual gifts and abilities. I feel compelled to write, teach, and counsel others about these healing experiences. All of my life, I have been guided by and attracted to supernatural aspects of life outside of my religious upbringing, such as ghosts, psychics, natural healers, and the nontraditional healing fields. I have always used a more holistic approach to find a harmonious, healing balance in life. I come from a long line of healers; my multicultural background is full of indigenous healers, and I've come to believe in generational cell memory and reincarnation.

Overcoming the pain, bleakness, bills, boredom, and brokenness of life seems to be a deep yearning that is hardwired into the soul of every person. As I understand it, the truth is that God makes something happen in us that we cannot make happen by ourselves—nor can any other

1

human being do it for us. God saved us, not because of the righteous things we have done but because of his mercy. He saved us through the washing of rebirth and renewal by the Holy Spirit, whom he generously poured out on us through Jesus Christ, our Savior (Titus 3:5–6). Only Jesus, the God-man, living in us through his Holy Spirit, can make this happen. This spirituality is freely available to us from God, and we can have it simply by asking for it. He is a great God, the great Hound of Heaven, who loves us and pursues us until we are exhausted by our attempts to flee from him, and we yield to his glorious way. The bottom line is that hurt people hurt people. Healing people in spiritual recovery help to heal people. We need each other, and we are connected by more than just flesh and blood.

> I alone am God, and beside me, there is no other. And thou shalt love the Lord thy God with all thy heart, and with all thy soul, and with all thy mind, and with all thy strength: this [is] the first commandment. (Mark 12:30)

I am writing based on my personal experiences and my walk with God because I asked him to help me to understand what I was experiencing. He showed me that what I was experiencing was real and not a part of our ancestors' imagination. The archangel Michael, Jesus, mother Mary, Buddha, Ganesh, and other spiritual warriors of my God helped me understand him, especially when I studied the Bible. It is the ultimate living grimoire about this planet, written by an omnipresence, the Alpha and Omega made flesh. He has ordained that I walk a different road that, sadly, few choose to follow (Matthew 7:13–14).

As a result, I have come home to myself. I know who I am and recognize my true feelings. This journey home is a process of feeling at ease within myself and feeling connected with my inner feelings and with that safe place of connection with I AM that I AM. It is the process of acknowledging that I am okay and worthy of God's love. Despite what is happening in this world, all is well. God is in control, and everything is happening as it has been preordained.

Bible

Basic Instructions before Leaving Earth

I had specifically asked God about these celestial beings, and my God answered my questions to my satisfaction. Almost all of my whys to God are now gone, and in their place is rest and peace for my soul. I have successfully died three times and—very unwillingly; fighting, kicking, and screaming—was sent back here. This is my story, and I am sticking to it.

Cultural domestication is a form of mind control.

When strange things happened in our family—and they happened all the time—we had a covert rule: never talk about them. I don't know how old I was when I learned this, but it was to a point where these strange things became normal. And normality is strange. If religion no longer serves your spiritual needs and purposes, and you are seeking a personal experience with God as you understand him, her, or it, this book is for you.

eternal. (Luke 21:33)

Some of the information may seem heretical, but as I was doing research through prayer, a lot of information just fell out. Coincidence? I don't think so. It is not my business how you perceive me. I don't expect you to believe what I say, nor do I care if you do, but a lot of my experiences will ring true to those whom God will appoint/has appointed, anointed, and empowered to your level of spiritual understanding. You are now ready to receive his spiritual food and to allow your individualized spiritual road map to guide you to your bliss. God says our journey through this world may take us along paths of pain and problems and deserts of deprivation and distress, like Jesus, his Son.

Jesus said challenging circumstances come and go, but I am constantly with you. I am writing the storyline of your life through good times and hard times. I can see the big picture—from before your birth to beyond the grave. I know exactly what you will be like when heaven becomes your forever-home. I am continually working to transform you into this perfect creation. You are royalty in my kingdom!

Don't be surprised by these fiery trials; take them in stride, trusting that the devil uses them to keep us under his control, and he has already been defeated. God/Jesus will never leave you or forsake you, even if you don't feel him at times, due to emotional upheavals. Thankfully, Jesus offers an alternative route. He is the one who offered to take our burdens on to himself, to carry our yokes so that we may find rest, love, hope, and even new life (Matthew 11:28–30). Yes, Jesus Christ is the one who will never leave my side, nor will he leave you. In due time, he will take us into the realm of his glory-light, which he has graciously shown me. If you are reading this book, God is calling you.

God Cannot Lie

When writing this book, I wanted to make sure that it was God's voice that I was hearing, and so he led me to seven different criteria to use for recognizing that I was truly hearing God's voice and not Satan's:

1. Does it make me more like Christ? What would Jesus do?
2. Full of mercy; finding the good and beauty; being sincere and genuine versus wearing a mask and

being a hypocrite (Philippians 2:5; 2 Corinthians 10:5; James 3:14–17).

3. Does my church family or spiritual or social group confirm it? (Ephesians 3:10; Proverbs 11:9, 17b).

4. Is it consistent with how God *shapes* me? Is it a good fit with who I am? (Ephesians 2:10; Romans 12:6). Shape:

   - spiritual gifts
   - heart
   - abilities
   - personality
   - experiences

5. Does it concern my responsibility? I am not God; therefore, God usually gives me insight, usually without my even knowing it. Someone else will normally confirm what God has told me to tell someone else.

6. Is it convicting rather than condemning? From God, correction is used to develop character and whatever needs to change. And God never attacks my values, Condemning is self-hate— feeling bad all the time and full of shame, guilt, and fear. This is not from God (Romans 8:1; Revelations 3:19).

7. Do I sense God's peace about it? (Philippians 4:6–7; Proverbs 22:17; John 8:47). Learn to recognize

God's voice: (Rick Warren, Saddleback Church, YouTube).

Life Begins with the Understanding of You

I am a teacher. I am also a student.

Here are the three most important questions that you will ever ask yourself as you journey throughout this world and get started on your path:

1. If we knew that we were going to succeed at whatever we did, what would we do or be?
2. If I had $100 million in the bank, what would I do or be?
3. If I knew I only had six months to live, what would I do or be? (Dr. Clint Rodgers, "Ancient Secrets of a Master Healer," Deeper Healing Solutions, Ted X Talks, Wilmington).

What is being said is not the truth; what is happening is.

I am a life force in a human body. We are angels of the Holy Spirit.

Jesus said, "You are fully known. I know absolutely everything about you and I love you with perfect unfailing love. It is in your relationship with me that you discover who you are" (1 Corinthians 13:12 HCSB).

I come from a line of doubting Thomases. I was born in Kansas City, Missouri. It is not called the Show-Me

State for nothing. My God chose to talk to me, personally, despite my desire and attempts to be a black coven witch, for which I was actively headhunted by a young coven at age thirteen.

God had archangel Michael, as I knew him, ferry me to the Hall of Akashic Records during my first death. Jesus showed up and held me in his arms for two weeks, while I was in a coma, as He allowed me to argue, fuss, and fight with him about whether I should stay on earth and finish my contract or go home to heaven with him. This was my second attempt at death. In the end, Jesus had his way, and I was infuriated that he didn't take me with him.

I had three interventions with mother Mary; I cussed her out in the first two meetings but submitted to her will on the third meeting, with much humility. She was healing me the whole time I was cussing her out, as a result of my unfinished mother issues. I also met death while in a military mental ward. She was so beautiful and left me with a beautiful gift in the form of a question—what did I learn from my experiences? God works best with skeptics and those with afflictions and drama in their lives; those who are overwhelmed with grief and disappointment, yet they kept the faith.

Some die, never having seen their promises brought into this reality. The Bible states that everyone who wants to live a godly life in Christ Jesus will be persecuted (2 Timothy 3:12). Famous biblical witnesses had the following shortcomings and deficiencies: Moses was a stutterer and a murderer. Rehab was a prostitute. Noah was an alcoholic. Abraham was a liar. Jacob was a deceiver. Samson was a womanizer. David was an adulterer and a murderer. Sara doubted God. Being flawed and damaged is the way my God prefers us, finding beauty in our brokenness and teaching us how powerful his unconditional love truly is (Isaiah 43:2; Hebrews 2:10).

All praise to the God and Father of our Lord Jesus Christ. He is the source of every mercy and the God who comforts us. He comforts us in all our troubles so that we can comfort others. When others are troubled, we will be able to give them the same comfort that God has given us. You can be sure that the more we suffer for Christ, the more God will shower us with his comfort through Christ (2 Corinthians 1:3–5).

God never promised us a rose garden, but, not unlike a caterpillar in a cocoon, we have to go through this process of struggles on this planet to become a beautiful butterfly, similar to our spiritual evolution in this dimension, world, realm, or matrix (1 Peter 3:14; 4:1; 5:10; 2 Corinthians 4:7; Colossians 1:24).

T. H. I. N. K.

Tell Him I Now Know
Everybody wants a miracle but nobody wants to in the
crisis that causes that miracle. Millions of Americans
are embarking on a search for the secret in their lives.
(Kantrowitz, 1994, 53). People are searching for God,
however they name him. They're looking for something
secret beyond themselves to anchor life and to give it
meaning amid its suffering and chaos. Pollster George
Gallup Jr. reported that 82 percent of Americans express
a need for greater intimacy with God, an increase of 24
percent in just four years, Gallup Poll (Gallup and Jones
2000).

All-knowing is the mindset of God, completely aware
of all there is, with the ability to know without experience.
This was not to be the mindset of man. Unknown in this
mindset, man must experience God's healing message of
self care:

Do not dwell on the past mistakes; you can learn from
them, but don't let it become your focus. You cannot undo
things that have already occurred. Instead of wishing
for the impossible, come to me and pour out your heart.
Remember that I am your refuge; trust in me at all times.

Don't let the busyness of your day drown out the voice
of your God. The devil will use busyness to keep you
from doing God's will and hearing his voice. The Lord is

faithful to all his promises and is loving toward all he has made. The Lord opposes all those who fall, and he lifts all who are bowed down. Those who have ears to hear, let them hear. Be creative; protect your quiet time with God. Slow down and listen. God is a chatterbox, and he has a wonderful sense of humor. All he's ever wanted to do is talk to you, love you, have a personal relationship with you, and bless you mightily. God says he loves us 310 times in the Bible.

Four Types of Love

There are four types of love in the Bible. The first one is called *storge*, which is an empathy bond. The second one is called *philia*—that is a friendship bond. The third one is called *eros*—that's a romantic love. The fourth kind of love is *agape*, or unconditional "God" love (C. S. Lewis, *The Four Loves*, 1960).

If you're not a morning person, God will meet you wherever you are—at lunch, on your drive to work, at the gym while working out. Spend some quiet time with him and listen. Call on him, and he'll show up. *Make sure it is God* by stating the power and the blood of Jesus Christ when you call on him. Sometimes, Satan shows up, masking himself as God and/or as angelic presence representing God (Matthew 6:24, 33; Psalm 46:10, 145; James 46:10; Isaiah 50).

Jesus said:

> I AM the RESURRECTION and the
> LIFE. He who believes in Me will live, even
> though he dies. I spoke this truth to Martha
> when her brother Lazarus had died, and she
> believe Me. Shortly thereafter, I command
> Lazarus to come out of his tomb, and he did.
> Even though he eventually died again—as
> all people do—he knew he would rise again
> to Life, as all believers will. (John 11:25,
> 43–44; 14:6 NKJV)

"I trust you, Jesus." Uttering these four words can brighten your day immediately. Dark clouds of worry are blown away by a simple, childlike trust (Psalm 62:8). Remember that I am your refuge. Trust me at all times. I can make a way where there appears to be no way. With me, all things are possible (Matthew 19:26).

Psychological, social, and political revolutions have not been able to transform the heart of darkness that lies deep in the breast of every human being. Amid a flood of self-fulfillment, there is an epidemic of depression, suicide, personal emptiness, and escapism. So obviously, the problem is a spiritual one. And so must be the cure (Dallas Willard, 1988, viii).

God in Christ is the Great Physician, the only one who is able to apply healing salve to our aching souls. God in Christ is the Great Redeemer, seeking and saving the lost, redeeming our darkened and desperate lives from greater travail. God in Christ is the Great Reconciliation, who forges new bonds and creates renewed relationships out of broken shards that otherwise would have only cut and wounded. God in Christ sends his Holy Spirit to us to shape in us the very same spirit of the one who sent him. Human suffering is universal; no one escapes; it is everywhere. Wealth, comfort, and medication do not separate us from pain; they only temporarily numb it. Therefore, we are hurting people in a broken world. Yes, suffering is also the royal road to experiencing the deeper things of God. C. S. Lewis referred to pain as God's megaphone, a gift nobody wants. Human beings lived in perfect harmony with God in the garden of Eden, but brokenness and suffering entered the world because of the fall (Genesis 3).

When hope is lost, when desires die, when dreams are shattered, we are broken. Some people give up and die in this brokenness, while others are desperately driven to search for a new hope. These are God-anointed wounded healers, who have suffered themselves and have allowed God to transform the "immature" them through their hardship. Unfortunately, far too many sufferers allow pain to blind them spiritually, to take away their faith and courage, and to bind up and freeze their hearts. However wounded, healers show a winsome spirit, express joy, speak wisdom, from their souls, which makes them wholly attractive to others, especially people in pain. This process is one of God's abiding miracles, one of the truly great paradoxical truths about life.

I decree and declare that this book is exalting the living God and moving you to invite the life and the love of Jesus Christ to permeate every facet of your life and your journey. This is my prayer, decree and declaration.

I AM that I AM. I am God, the Alpha and the Omega, the God most high, possessor of heaven and earth, and you are not—neither is Satan.

This may seem harsh, but it's actually a blessed dose of reality. In the garden of Eden, Satan tempted Eve with the very same desire that caused him to fall from heaven—to be like God, usurping God's divine position. Eve succumbed to this temptation, as did Adam. Since that time, the sin nature in people promised them to act as if they were God, trying to control everything, judging everyone else when circumstances didn't go as they liked.

Remembering that you are not God helps you to live in freedom. You don't take responsibility for matters that are beyond your control, which includes most matters.

If you let go of everything that is not your responsibility, you are free from caring for unnecessary burdens. And you can be more effective in areas where you do have some control. Moreover, you can pray about all your concerns, trusting in God's sovereignty. Bring Him your prayers with thanksgiving; present your requests to Him.

Living this way will shield you from anxiety and bless you with the peace that transcends all understanding (Sarah Young, *Jesus Always*, 157).

The Devil Is a Liar

Satan is a master in highlighting our sense of unworthiness and hidden sins. He also attempts to mimic Jesus to fool God's anointed by using visions, anger, oppression, and possessions as gateways to infiltrate our minds and bodies, to become guest houses and hotels for his demonic spirits (Joel 2:27–31; Matthew 24:24; Mark 13; 2 Corinthians 11:4; Acts 16:16–17). You might ask yourself, "Am I relying on my own personal experience, rather than the Bible, and does it go against the Bible?"

These are the biggest lies Satan tells God's children. The devil told me I'm not loved. He told me no one would ever understand me. He told me that men will always leave me. He told me that I will forever be alone and that my God doesn't care about me.

The devil is a liar. I told Satan, "The Lord rebukes you, and so do I. Satan, you have been defeated by the power of the blood of Jesus Christ, and in the name of Jesus Christ, I command you to flee," and he will flee. I told him, "Greater is he who is in me than he that is in the world. I will never be alone. Men may come and go, but my God will never leave me or forsake me. He knows my name. I trust my God with my life for all of my days. He holds my hand." This is what I declared. It is my story, and I am sticking to it.

Man Looks at Outward Man; God Looks at the Heart

Ask Jesus to train you in trusting him more consistently. Well-developed trust enables you to go across treacherous terrain without stumbling. The more challenging your journey, the more frequently you need to voice your confidence in Jesus.

You can pray, "Lord, I trust in your unfailing love." This short prayer reminds Jesus to remind you that he is with you, and he is taking care of you. He loves you forever—rejoice, beloved. Jesus is truly worthy of your thankfulness and trust (Psalm 16:11; 52:8).

Jesus's Divine Purpose

I believe my divine purpose is to end domestic violence, child abuse, and all of its devastating components in my lifetime by opening up spiritually and culturally based healing homes and centers, to be used as a platform for healing all over the world. I was raised Baptist, born guilty. I was forced to go to church until age sixteen, enduring all kinds of spiritually abusive scenarios inside these man-made churches, the rules of which were ordained by the rulers of this world, not God. Inside these church homes, I was told that according to God, I was filthy rags in God's sight, not worthy of forgiveness. I was not to pray for myself but for others only.

My thought was, *Then why pray?* To me, that was taking humility to a nuclear-destructive level of human conditioning, with the same impact as shame, running a quick second only to guilt (symbolic violence, historically used as tools to keep people oppressed and controllable).

For a very long time, I couldn't tell the difference between the words *humility, shame,* and *guilt* and their true spiritual meanings. I couldn't live with that concept of a "loving God" by my mother's and father's definition and version of God. It was an oxymoronic term that didn't make sense to me.

In my dealings with religious leaders, I learned that if the preachers had not experienced or heard of similar experiences, all of my encounters were from Satan, not God. They did not do their due diligence in researching the Bible like I did. I have found this a quick go-to answer when they didn't know. As a result, I have found myself in a no-win situation with religious leaders and their organizations, including their interpretations of the Bible, in which I was to accept their answers without question.

Many mental health professionals, including some of the field's leading lights, have characterized religious people, and especially Christians, as simple-minded, easily controlled, and thoroughly diluted (Ellis 1971;

Freud 1927; Watson 1924, 1983). Though no empirical evidence exists to support these claims, faith has been viewed, from this naturalistic, anti-supernatural mindset, as something pathological. Christians are broad-brushed as manipulated masses who are intolerant, living in denial, and even dangerous to the commonwealth, due to their fanatical fundamentalist beliefs. "I don't believe a Christian could ever be a professional counselor," one woman stated in a class that was considering the role of religious and spiritual values in counseling.

Christians will push the toxic faith positions on clients who are seeking help, especially their view about homosexuality and abortion (Clinton 1998, 30). I rejected religion—the beliefs, values, and practices of various established religions—but not the Bible, God, Jesus, or the Holy Spirit. It was the right move for me and Jesus both. I was seeking a relationship with a higher force, being, power, or God. Satan is just an over-glorified angel that got fired and demoted to the earth realm because he believed his own lies, and he forgot that God made him.

The god of New Age spirituality seems pantheistic, universal, hyper-tolerant, and impersonal force that exists in all; it is all that exists. This can easily lends itself to a free-wheeling, anything-goes definition of spirituality that devolves into the subjective, self-focused cycle of spirituality.

My spirituality is centered around studying the Bible, God, Jesus, and the Holy Spirit, and I have a very loving relationship with them, all living in my life today. For many seekers, rational thought is denied, as more and more people look inside themselves to find fulfillment and enlightenment. Being a very sensitive, inquisitive, and intuitive child, youth, adult, and, now, elder, my questions about my strange experiences were and still are answered fully by my God.

I believe my experiences are gifts of the spirit, as I understand it, based on my thoroughly wonderful personal relationship with my God and researching the Bible for myself, including reading it front to back about four times throughout this existing lifetime. In my search for clarity, I turned my back on religion and went straight to my God, as I understand him, based on spiritual truths I had uncovered in my search for truth. Based upon my personal experiences with churches, religion is a basic application of our biblical knowledge to life. Too many churches are in denial and will not admit they need help.

If a child goes to the church leader or elder and says, "I am being molested at home," and the church leader starts quoting scriptures, how effective is that to the child? This, sadly, is a real-case scenario. And the child was blamed for the molestation. This type of scenario happens more often than not. Thus, the churches are losing our most valuable resource and it is seen as an impotent example of God by our children.

I believe that once the church is honest, accountable, receptive, and helpful to others in a small group context, true sanctification can take place; the church can become more caring and restorative. I personally believe that church leaders need to be certified as Bible-knowledge counselors. I feel that some of the leaders lack empathy; they are burned out, have compassion fatigue, and are seduced by the all-mighty dollar. It is no wonder we question the authenticity of some of these religious leaders, especially while widows, elders, and single parents and children become poorer and poorer in spirit, due to their sense of separation. I believe, according to the Bible, that the church's primary job was to look after this targeted group, not steal or take money from them.

Ask Me to Increase Your Thankfulness

Jesus said,

> This will brighten your day and open your heart to me. Seek to see me in your circumstances. Look for signs of my unseen presents as you walk along the path of life gratefulness. It's not only your heart that you should open but also your eyes. When you know me intimately, you can find me in my right tiny details as well as in the big picture of your life. Take time to notice all my blessings small and large and to thank

me for them this practice will help you enjoy my many gifts. (Colossians 2:6–7 NASB)

I had three questions for God:

1. Who am I?
2. Why am I here?
3. What is my purpose?

I received these messages from him:

First, he told me, "Lou, be convicted."

Second, my God told me, "Make me what you need me to be, so that you will know that I AM that I AM." (I am not that deep intellectually, and that answer didn't come from me). His answers to my questions were, "You are my beloved, and you volunteered to come here." Second, he indicated that I am here with others to end the cycle of domestic violence and its impact on our society.

I am here to let a man know that until he makes it right with women, with inequality issues, we will always be in a state of domestic violence and chaos for our world and our future generations, in all of its components. Then the Book, The Holy Mother Mary is God, introduces the greatest mysteries which have been obscured from humanity for thousands of years. This unfoldment of the truth that we all have been searching for is revealed to you not only in the author's words, but from the actual words of God...leading credence to demonic conspiracy (Kelly, K.P., 1957,1ˢᵗ ed 2013.

Another mind blowing spiritual book called (E.V.O.W). Enlightened Voice Of Women, is something that everyone may want to get their hands on. It speaks volumes to your soul. Women you truly learn who we are through spiritual eyes. To men, it explains who you are, where you came from and what you're ordained to become.

My purpose is to be a people-builder, looking for opportunities to encourage others, to bring out the best in them and help them accomplish their dreams, to call out their seeds of greatness, to rise higher and become all God has created them to be, and to end the cycle of domestic violence in its entirety.

Harvesting the Good

Change your thinking; change your life.

> With every deed you are sowing a seed, though the harvest you may not see. (Ella Wheeler Wilcox)

Some of my names are wonderful counselor (Isaiah 9:6; Romans 8:38–39; Psalm 37:48). I understand you far better than you understand yourself. Come to me with your problems and insecurities, seeking my counsel.

The light of my loving presence you can see yourself, as you are radiantly lovely in my brilliant righteousness. Though my righteousness is perfect, you will continue to struggle with your imperfection—and others—as long as you live in this world. Still, your standing with me is secure. Nothing in all creation will separate you from my love. A wonderful counselor is not only extremely good at helping people but also is able to inspire delight or pleasure. Delight yourself in me, beloved, and I will give you the desires of your heart.

One of my greatest challenges in life is when I speak about concepts. I want my words and examples to be consistent, clear, concise, and understood by all—well, at least by the majority of my audience. That is one of the major reasons for enrolling in universities with God's blessings—so I can face my giants with confidence and open up healing homes for at-risk youth who are affected by domestic violence and all of its inherent constituents.

As a lifelong learner, I pray that God keeps me green so I can continue to grow because we all know that, like fruit, when we are ripe, we rot. In Genesis, the human race was made by and for God. Human beings live in perfect harmony with God.

As a result of Adam and Eve's sins in the garden of Eden, brokenness and suffering entered the world because of the fall. Genesis 3 and Job 5:7 remind us, "Man is born to trouble as surely as sparks fly upward." Our eyes are blinded to God's love because the pain and trouble—human suffering—is universal; no one escapes. Ain't nobody getting out of here alive. Wealth, comfort, and medication do not separate us from the pains of this planet; they only temporarily numb it.

Death is not the absence of life but the triumph over life, the prize for having gone through life's turmoil, its ups and downs.

This world is the boot camp of fear, shame, guilt, and death on a physical, emotional, mental, and spiritual level. One of Satan's biggest lies to humankind is that death looms over us, and losing life is the ultimate failure. The truth is, we are here to overcome those issues so that we can be wholly acceptable to God when we go to heaven and live with Jesus. God is so mighty. He is using Satan and his minions to strengthen us and to get us ready for ascension purposes.

It won't be easy, but it will be so worth it for those who are seeking truth. Just hang in there, baby. Change is coming. My God doesn't want us to worry about a thing. He wants us to replace shame, guilt, and fear (Satan's tools of destruction and death for us) with faith, trust, and the love of Jesus Christ, I AM that I AM, made flesh.

I have been mandated to share this information with you. Don't trust me. Do your research. I have put plenty in this book to start you on your journey.

Pray about this book and the information it imparts. Allow the Holy Spirit to guide you, teach you, and lead you down the path of righteousness so that you may live abundantly, victoriously, and with explicable joy and peace as you walk with Jesus and God. I call him Father, Abba, or Papa—that is how close I feel to him. He introduced himself to me as I AM that I AM. Other people have different names, such as Most High God, Allah, the Great One, the Great Entity, solar logos, the Great Initiator, King of kings and Lord of lords, Haroutiun Saraydarian Christ, the avatar of sacrificial love.

In Exodus 6:3, when Moses first spoke with God, God said to Moses, "I used to appear to Abraham, Isaac, and Jacob as El Shaddai but I did not make myself known to them by my name YHWH."

In my world, God's presence is more real than the flesh-and-blood people around me. God does not want his chosen people to be ignorant of his Word and will or ignorant of our enemy.

> Study to show thyself approved unto God, a workman that needed the not to be ashamed, rightly dividing the word of truth. But shun profane and vain babbling: for they will increase unto more unholiness. (2 Timothy 2:15)

How are you going to fight a battle if you don't know who your enemy is? In the end, it is not about us; it is about Jesus/God made flesh.

Shortly before my crucifixion, I taught my disciples; "I am the Way, the Truth, and the Life." I am everything you could need—for this life and the next. I am the Treasure that encompasses all treasures. This truth can simplify your life immensely! I am the answer to all your struggles, the Joy that pervades all time and circumstances. I can make hard times bearable and good times utterly delightful. So come to Me just as you are, beloved; share more and more of your life with Me. Rejoice as you journey with Me—the Way who guides you always and the Resurrection who gives you Eternal life. (John 14:1 NKJV; Colossians 2:2–3; Matthew 11:28)

Ride the Wild Tiger, Ride

God is here, and there is a plan. It is in your relationship with God that you discover who you are.

A closed mind is like a closed fist—it can neither open nor receive. For skeptics and critical thinkers and scientific researchers who are entrenched in empirical thinking, God is asking you, "Shall man, gifted with the power of reason, unthinkingly follow an adhered-to dogma, creeds, and hereditary beliefs, which will not bear the analysis of reason in this century of enlightened reality?"

This is your time to make your mark in this century of life and renewal. Sciences and arts, industry, and invention are being reformed. Laws and ethics are being reinstitute and, reorganized. The world of thought is being regenerated. Sciences of former ages and philosophies of the past are useless today. Today, our world demands new methods of solutions; world problems are without precedents. Old ideas and modes of thought are becoming obsolete. Ancient laws and archaic ethical systems are not meeting the requirements of our modern conditions.

This is the century of a new life, the century of the revelation of the reality, and, therefore, the greatest of all centuries. Will we allow tyrannical rulers of former governments to answer the call for freedom that has risen from the heart of humanity, including your sons and daughters, in this cycle of illumination? Shall blind imitations of ancestral forms and theological interpretations continue to guide and control the religious life and spiritual development of humanity today?

This is God's challenge to you. Life is like a wild tiger. You can either lie down and let it lay its paw on your head, or sit on its back and ride it. Without question, this will not satisfy men of science, for when they find premise or conclusion contrary to present standards of proof and without real foundation, they reject that which has been formally accepted as standard and correct and move forward from new foundations.

Therefore, if the nations of the world forsake imitations and investigate the reality underlying the revealed Word of God, they will agree and become reconciled, for reality is one and not multiple.

Expect the best. Convert problems into opportunities Be dissatisfied with the status quo. Focus on where you want to go instead of where you're coming from. Most importantly, decide to be happy, knowing it's an attitude, a choice, a habit gained from daily practice and not a result or payoff (Denis Waitley).

Why the Bible Is Number One

The Bible is the most historically accurate document in history. The Bible is the only accurate prophetic book of past and future events in the world. Even though the Bible does not contain scientifically inaccurate statements, atomic scientists have found the God particle in the Higgs boson. In 2012, scientists confirmed the detection of the long-sought Higgs boson, also known by its nickname, the "God particle," at the Large Hadron Collider (LHC), the most powerful particle accelerator on the planet (Kenny Barfield 1988, 9–10).

The God particle helps give mass to all elementary particles that have mass, such as electrons and protons. The Bible goes further in that it foresees scientific discoveries before they were known to the world at large. During the time the Bible was being composed, there was much superstition and ignorance concerning the nature and function of the universe, the Bible being a notable exception. We do not find the biblical writers committing the same type of errors as their contemporaries.

Everything that makes up the universe (stars, planets, etc.,) can be considered cells in the body of God, cells that compose the body of this huge source, and we are nothing more than the tiniest cell in the circulation process (just like the children's book *Horton Hears a Who*). Although we may be something so minute, we are not insignificant because in our evolution and growth, it is possible for us to constantly rise toward the morass of life. Our universe is a highly complex organism, living in many dimensions at the same time, composed of layers and layers of consciousness that relates to all the other organisms within it. It has the power to create and relate to all of these at the same time, individually—what we have called a collective. This is so because we collectively have thought it into existence by intent.

We are all part of the collective, the one, the great central sun, the source God—whatever you wanna call it. Curiosity is not strictly a human trait; maybe God is the source of our desire to explore came from. we all as part of the fourth as co-creators help it begin to create. We helped create out of nothing or out of dust, as it is reported in several legends, and stars, planets, rocks, streams, plants, animals, and humans came into being. Then we decided—or were told—to go and have these things and to report back to the source what this was like. It is said that it is all nothing but an illusion. If this is correct, then it is held together by our collective perception. We have helped to think it into existence, and our combined perception holds it there.

I was wondering if there could be, among all the so-called revelations of the world religions, one document that is untouched by the foibles and fallacies of men; one record that reveals an accurate understanding of men and nature; one collection of writing that holds an immutable relationship to scientific truth. One book and only one can meet these qualifications; it is known as the Bible. God is the greatest scholar, and master of the universe, the Great Architect, Creator, and controller of all there is. God spoke the world into existence. He formed people in his image and gave them eternal souls.

WHAT DOES LIFE ETERNAL MEAN?

Eternal means forever. Soul is a dimension that stores energy. You can imagine yourself as many pixelated boxes, forming into one existence, which is you. In our age, most of us would use spiritual energy or life force to form a connection with the universe. Eternal means forever.

He created beauty in the world and throughout the universe. He is infinitely more brilliant than the greatest genius imaginable. His wisdom is unsearchable, and his love is unfailing, despite all the evidence-based facts.

"Blessed are those who have learned to acclaim [me]" (Psalm 89:15). God just blows my mind when I ponder his glorious greatness. I am personally proclaiming the excellence of he who called me out of darkness into his marvelous light (1 Peter 2:9). God is encouraging you to get out of your head and go to your heart because we have three brains (heart, mind, and soul or stomach), not one. This is not the natural inclination of humankind; it is something we need to learn and practice, beginning with our thoughts.

Those who are spiritually inclined notice the number three. God told me that numbers were a language, and this is how he talks and shows hard-core science that he is truly God. I base this on my sixty-one years of strenuous and arduous research, seeking truth and the real God of my fathers, not the God that man told me to believe in. Man's interpretation of God left me feeling not freed but chained to Satan's rules and feeling suicidal. The flesh of man is hostile toward God (Romans 8:7–9). The mind governed by the flesh is hostile to God; it is not subject to God's law, nor can it do so.

Satan's purpose is to lie, steal, kill, and destroy us—that's his nature. He is a master at utilizing doubt, shame, fear, and guilt, which is his greatest skill that he uses on God's anointed. God's nature is to be faithful and trustworthy. God utilizes patience and kindness and does not envy. It does not boast. It is not proud. It does not dishonor others. It is not self-seeking. It is not easily angered. It keeps no record of wrongs. Love does not delight in evil but rejoices with the truth. It protects trust, always hopes, and preserves; love never fails. God is love (1 Corinthians 13:4–8). If God ain't in it, is it love?

As God's anointed, we will judge the angels, and he was and is still pissed. Plus, Satan's time here is limited. The war in heaven was fought; he and his minions lost. God won! The evil one knows what his future holds so he doesn't have anything to lose in getting many people to go to hell with him and especially God's anointed, who have given Satan power over their lives. These are some of his last acts of disobedience. He is flipping the bird or blowing a raspberry to God (Matthew 24:5; 1 John 3).

This is not your battle to fight. Stop worrying, let go, and let God. Allow the Holy Spirit to guide you, and keep talking to God. Ask him to fight this battle on your behalf.

> We have nothing to fear but fear itself. (Franklin D. Roosevelt)
>
> Death is not the opposite of life but a part of it. (Hiroki Murakami)

Most humans have been taught to be afraid of death, and we are violent because of that. I am here to tell God's people that the devil is a liar. From several personal experiences with death, it is the graduation from this boot camp called earth. God told me we all volunteered for this mission here on earth. Some of us are human beings, some of us are not, and some of us are not from here but visitors; others are celestial watchers. When meeting them, try not to act out of fear. Call on the Lord if you are afraid to help you overcome things that keep you chained to Satan's will. Satan creates illusions for us to live in confusion. You will never be free if you live by what you see. Man looks at the outward appearance, but God looks at the heart. If you have fulfilled your contact from this temporary dimension, death is a resting place to remember and to recover from this battlefield. You will have accumulated knowledge, wisdom, and information, gained from this dimension, which will be added on your next soul journey of ascension. All this suffering we go through strengthens our spiritual muscles of faith, trust, devotion, and glory to God/Jesus, in preparation to live in his kingdom. We are under contract and co-creating with God and are co-collaborators in fulfilling his will. Where your treasure is, your heart will be.

From those glimpses, other pieces of my God's masterpiece and plan are seen. Mohandas Karamchand Gandhi—lawyer, political ethicist, prophet—demonstrated nonviolence. This great soul fought for independence for his people and was assassinated on January 30, 1948. Dr. Martin Luther King Jr. talked about God's promises and dreams coming to pass and fought for civil and economic rights for all citizens. This Baptist minister, inspired by Christ, advocated nonviolence and civil disobedience. He was assassinated on April 4, 1968. Diana, Princess of Wales, acted very Christlike. She was the "people's princess" and a philanthropist. She promoted human welfare worldwide. Her sincere and genuine love for humanity was self-evident by her actions. She was killed in a fatal car accident on August 8, 1997.

Coincidences? I don't think so. Connect the dots. Their life stories are similar to the situational comparison that led to the assassination/crucifixion of Christ.

You are a letter from me, written not with ink but with the spirit of the living God on the tablet of your heart (2 Corinthians 3:3). These individuals were his living letter to us.

I am a kingdom kid and subject to kingdom principles.

My mystical experiences go beyond ordinary sense perception, revealing deeper truths about myself/ ourselves and our relationship with the divine. Mystics have been ridiculed, persecuted, and even killed for their beliefs, but their teachings endure, urging us to look beyond the ordinary—and into the eyes of God (*The Road to Armageddon: A Spiritual Documentary*; Psalm 121).

HAIL—Honesty, Authenticity, Integrity, and Love

To me, these are the cornerstones of my covenant with God. His grace and mercy rescued me and brought me through. Because you are one of his followers, the Holy Spirit is in you. He equips and empowers you to do far more than you could ever do on your own. Don't be intimidated by challenging circumstances or tough times. The third person of the Godhead lives inside you. The Holy Spirit writes on the tablet of your heart, not only to bless you but also to draw others to me when you are with people who don't know Jesus.

The Holy Spirit can make you a living letter from me for those who don't know Jesus. When you invite the Holy Spirit into your life, he brings the gospel truths alive through you. You can do much more than you think possible when you walk in the way of Jesus by asking the helper to strengthen you as you go, step by step, with me. So much of man's rationalization/coping style is, "Don't confuse me with the facts."

Satan Wants to Keep Us Ignorant

One of the best examples of how our society and other societies are kept ignorant of Satan's machinations is the eye-popping, connect-the-dots documentary on a biblical conspiracy, *The Exodus Decoded*.

The one who practices sin is of the devil, for the devil has been practicing from the beginning. The Son of God appeared for this purpose—to destroy the works of the devil (1 John 3:8). Our adversaries are the world and Satan, who is the prince of this world.

The world around me is not my home; each day, it becomes more of a reflection of Satan, its prince. I am not ignorant to Satan's devices, and I understand that the world is designed for my destruction. The allurement of pleasure and the temptations that cross my eyes are for the purpose of robbing me of everything I have inherited through Christ. Every trap, every lust, and the pride that is in the world are set against me on all sides. Satan's minions The demon of rage, the demon of narcissism, the incubus and succubus demons, and the lord demon, self-intelligence (I am right and smarter than God). mission is to steal kill and destroy and is running most of the entertainment industry today.

The hope that I have is in patiently walking according to your Word, God, and staying firm to the covenant I have made with you. The world cannot strip me of my authority, but I can hand it over. I will not be deceived by what I see or hear or how I feel. If it is not of God, then it is for my destruction. Help me, Lord, to see the spirit behind the temptation. The Word tells me that Satan came to steal, kill, and destroy, but Jesus comes that I may have life and have it more abundantly.

Ignorance Is the Hardest Disability to Overcome

This is my story. I am being guided by my God to write this book for those who can see a great beauty in

Christ and want to express that beauty by living a life of sacrificial love. I will use my family tree and familial conditioning that has impacted all aspects of to whom the world was trying to mold me—into their image. But God had other plans. I believe God listens to all prayers, and he answers. I can only say that he has been a faithful and trustworthy partner in all my endeavors in which I have asked him to collaborate. He answered my questions about my sexuality and getting healed from the generational familial curses of incest, pedophilia, every aspect of domestic violence, and child abuse, including throwing off the mantle of shame of spiritual abuse.

> If one desires a change one must be that change before that change can take place. (Gita Bellin)

We create our experiences of what we focus on. Try something different.

Martin Luther was a German professor of theology, a composer, a priest and a monk, and a seminal figure in the Protestant Reformation. He was ordained to the priesthood. In 1507, he came to reject several teachings and practices of the Roman Catholic Church. In particular, he disputed the views on indulgences. He was persecuted because he pointed out to the religious community the abuses that were taking place. Acting on his belief, he wrote the "Disputation on the Power and

Efficacy of Indulgences," also known as "The Ninety-Five Theses"—a list of questions and propositions for debate. He defiantly nailed a copy to the door of a Wittenberg church. It resulted in a movement against those abuses. People were able to understand what they were. Where people would pay money to the church to take care of their sins and sanctioned them to commit sins in the future, Martin Luther said it was wrong. As a result, he ran for his life to Wartburg Castle in Germany, where he sought sanctuary from the vengeance of the church. During this time, he experienced satanic attacks and discouragement, yet despite that, within two weeks, he was able to translate from Hebrew, written in ancient Greek, the New Testament into a German-language Bible. The New Testament was first published in 1522 in the complete Bible, containing the Old and New Testaments, with Apocrypha in 1534.

I'm just a nobody, trying to tell everybody about somebody who can save anybody.

I confronted and educated my family, prayerfully. We are all victims and abusers and speak about it. It is my major testimony to God's grace—that obstacle and mountain in my life. All abuse done to me was mostly done in secrecy, hidden and justified behind the mask of spiritual abuse. The kicker is, when you walk with Christ, the Holy Spirit comes in and convicts your heart and challenges you to go outside your comfort zone.

I had to go to my primary abusers. Some I confronted about my abuse as a child, and others, I had to ask for forgiveness, not for their sake but my sake. The harm done to me in the past no longer has any power over me, and I don't pour that poison out on others. Jesus helped me to let go of a whole warehouse of past baggage that no longer served my higher purpose or good and replaced them with gifts I didn't know I had. Being attentive, open to the urging or gut feeling of Jesus, and being obedient, my gifts of the Holy Spirit were and are the desires of my heart. The curse of victimization no longer holds power over me. I have been freed.

My God is so honorable and patient and sensitive to us. He will not intervene in our lives unless we ask him and let him into our lives (Matthew 7:7–8). My God's majestic greatness and his gentle humility gives us everything we need. He wants us to know that because we live in a broken world, it can be hard to remember that we are royalty, adopted into the family of the King of kings.

What does that mean? God promises that we will live victoriously. We were created in his image. We have the DNA of winners, wearing crowns of favor. God said royal blood flows through our veins, and as such, we are the heads never the tails, above never beneath. We are destined to live in victory with supernatural purpose, passion, and praise to God.

What is eternal life? Eternal is endless, everlasting, and perpetual, implying lasting or going on without ceasing.

That which is eternal is, by its nature, without beginning or end: God, the eternal Father. That which is endless never stops but goes on continuously, as if in a circle, an endless succession of years.

How do you get to heaven? "He who does the will of the father who is in heaven" (Matthew 7:21).

Some people say there are many ways to get into heaven. In religious or mythological cosmology, there are seven heavens, referred to as seven levels or divisions of heaven. Who will be given eternal life?

"My sheep hear my voice, and I know them, and they follow me: and I gave them to them eternal life; and they shall never perish" (John 10:27–28). Jesus references a personal, heart-to-heart relationship with his anointed.

Does everyone automatically get to heaven? Every human being is, by nature, a sinful being, as a result of being born on this earth. The Bible says that our efforts at doing good deeds are not acceptable in the sight of God (Ephesians 2:8–9). God alone is holy. God alone is good. So God has made a way for sinful human beings to enter into his heaven (John 3:15–18).

This book will attempt to give you the answers that you may have thought about but never dared to ask out loud. In prayerful and diligent research, I have found a large library of books from various religions that validate what I am relaying to you. Please seek God's guidance in all that you do as you embark on this awesome personalized journey. Satan has been busy. His time is limited. He is not worried about his minions. He is after God's anointed and is using every tool in his bag of tricks to get us on his side.

If you're having difficulties in your search, as I did, do not be surprised if strange and weird situations, people, machines, and especially unreliable fear you've never encountered before occur in your life. That's Satan, trying to stop you from finding out the truth, and that is a good thing because you're on the right track. This is why God tells us not to trust men who are ruled by Satan.

God created us to have a loving, communicative relationship with him. We were to be immortal. God doesn't want us to feel alone, but Satan does so he can manipulate us. God wants us to think for ourselves and become partners in Christ embracing joy in his presence.

Believe it or not, there are people in this world/realm who are addicted to pain, suffering, chaos, sickness, and trouble and are committed to evil. I can say that from my own experience, at age thirteen. I knew exactly what I was walking into by joining a black witches coven. As a result of the spiritual abuse, accompanied by the domestic abuse and violence I experienced and suffered in my family under the guise of spirituality, I felt righteously angry. I wanted revenge. I wanted power. I wanted justice. I hated, with a passion, the God who man told me he was. All those who had hurt me in the past, whether they knew it or not, were going to suffer. I was going to have a front-row seat, watching my revenge unfold by becoming a black coven witch.

Justice is what I called it. I felt righteously angry over my plight in life. At around age thirteen, I lived on the outskirts of Seattle in a very expensive bedroom community. We were the only blacks in our town. In my junior high school, I had President Nixon's sister-in-law as my math teacher. My family was one of the only blacks going to that school at the time.

There was a coven of black witches at the school, and when they walked down the hallways, everybody moved out of their way. Not even the principals or the teachers would bother them. They all wore black clothes and black capes. It was normal in our school, and nobody bothered them. These were politicians' and lawyers' children. These children never talked to anybody. They stayed to themselves. They were very powerful. I quickly realized that they had power over the whole school, and I found that highly seductive. While I was observing them, I did not realize that they were observing me too.

A group of the coven members (around three) cornered me while I was in the bathroom and asked me if I want to be a part of the coven. I didn't hesitate; I said yeah, and they asked me to meet them in the woods at midnight that night, behind the school. They said they were going to show me how powerful the being they worshipped was. I had done my due diligence on the history of black and white witches in my independent research and study in search for my religion of my choosing, so I knew exactly what to expect with the black witches' coven.

Because of God's divine intervention during this scenario, I have a foggy memory of everything that took place, but I do have snapshots of the situation. I still can't remember the girls who asked me to join the coven. It's almost like anything connected to that situation—specific names, dates—was blotted out of my mind. Just pictures is all I have. I was taken deep into the woods, into an area that had been used for rituals. There were stumps of trees that had been clear-cut, seemingly for their rituals. Candles lit the place. It was midnight. I was not scared, but I was determined. I think there were seven coven members older than me. I was the only freshman present.

They had me sit on a stump, and it was lit by candles surrounding me. They told me to be still and that something was gonna happen. They left me there in the middle of the woods, with the candles lit all around me. Then, all of a sudden, something dark and shadowy came out of the woods, and it blew out all the candles. Something happened. It was like a big fight was going on in front of me. Then I heard a loud, clear voice in my right ear: "You need to leave, and you need to leave now," and I did.

I don't remember how I got home, but the next day, those girls left me alone. They didn't come near me. They didn't even look at me. It was almost like it never had happened, and that was the really strange part.

> For great is thy mercy toward me: and thou
> hast delivered my soul from the lowest
> hell. ... But thou, O Lord, art a God full
> of compassion. and plenteous in mercy and
> truth. (Psalm 86:13, 15)

My chosen people are holy and dearly loved. I know
that you are neither perfect nor sinless, but you are indeed
holy in my sight. I have wrapped you in the radiance of my
righteousness. I love you, Lord, for your mercy has never
left me. Your goodness is running after me so no fire came
to burn me. No battle can turn me, no mountain can stop
me, because you hold my hand.

> I am walking in your victory because your
> power is within me. No giant can defeat me
> because you hold my hand. I am his own.
> (Psalm 23:6)

When God, Jesus, or the Holy Spirit talks to me, their
voices/energies are male. But in my dream time, I report
to a female energy. She is my spiritual supervisor and
guardian angel. God has permitted me to remind you
of who you are—his children. You know who you are in
this fallen world. "Ye are of God, little children, and have
overcome them: because greater is he that is in me than
he that is the world" (1 John 4:4).

Regardless of what happens in your life, you are on a
winning team. I believe that Jesus is on the way back to

the world of men to renew in our hearts the greater hope, a greater faith, in a greater love.

One of his names is wonderful counselor. He understands us far, far better than we understand ourselves, and he wants us to come to him with our problems and insecurities, seeking his counsel. He is my strength when I am weak. The great I AM provides for me. In our weakness, he can mold us to God's will. In the light of his loving presence, you can see yourself as you are—radiantly lovely in his brilliant righteousness. You will continue to struggle with imperfection (yours and others') as long as you live in this world. Still, your standing with Jesus is secure. Nothing in all creation can separate you from his love. A wonderful counselor helps you to recognize truth and to live according to it.

Jesus was born and came into the world to testify to the truth. He is not only extremely good at helping people, but he also is able to inspire and to give delight or pleasure, giving you the desires of your heart. (Isaiah 9:6; Romans 8:38–39; Psalm 37:4).

Most important, with guidance from my higher power, as I understand him, I would encourage and challenge you to seek God's will and stay in communication with him daily. Love God; trust his Son, Jesus; and allow the Comforter, the Holy Spirit, to guide you, teach you, protect you, and lead you through this fallen and broken world. We have already won the victory through Jesus's death and resurrection. Jesus is the eternal victor, and we share in his triumph. No matter how much adversity you encounter on your journey to heaven, ultimately, nothing and no one can prevail against you because you belong to Jesus forever. As a follower of Jesus Christ, you have a guilt-free status guaranteed. You are in good hands with I AM that I AM.

What the Love of God Means to Me

He's never let me down. He's never broke my heart. He's never let me fall, so I give my heart to you. Jesus, take the wheel (Psalm 89:15).

My initiation to God/Jesus was at the age of five. I sincerely sought him. He has been faithful and trustworthy and still is, even now. Throughout my journey with Jesus, he has never let me down. He has never forgotten me or let me go, and he has been there every step of the way. Jesus said, "Your relationship with me transcends all your circumstances." This is why you can praise me and enjoy my presence amid the darkest difficulties. To find me in such times, you have to exert your faith. I am always near. As a Christian, you live on two planes simultaneously: the natural world, where adverse situations abound, and the supernatural world, where I reign supreme.

Your trust-muscles empower you to experience my presence, even in your hardest times. Trials can both strengthen your faith and help you discern how much you trust me. I want you to work on strengthening your trust-muscles. One way is to fill your mind and heart with scripture. Another is to seek my face continually. Instead of getting stuck in introspection, turn your thoughts toward me. Make it a practice to affirm your faith in me frequently, whether you're feeling confident or inadequate. Remember that your adequacy rests in your relationship with me.

I make you ready for anything and equal to anything by infusing inner strength into you! As I look back over my life and experiences—oh, my goodness! The rest of my journey with him was sketchy, at best, because I made mistakes, time after time. Through pain, suffering, anger, and self-destruction, I started to believe that he truly cared about me, and slowly, like a frightened deer, I trusted him.

Because of the free-will choices available to me, I was my own worst enemy. Because he spoke over me—even when I didn't see, even couldn't feel it, even when I didn't know at times—I knew Jesus's word and his love never fails. He has always showed that he cares for me and you, if we let him. I am so grateful for the victory he has won. I could go on and on about his grace and mercy. I'm going to just praise you, Lord, with a supernatural attitude of gratitude, thanksgiving, and thankfulness flowing from my heart.

Men do not learn much from the lessons of history
and that is the most important lesson of history.
—Aldous Huxley

Sacred Orchard

The reshaping of values in the process of society today forces modern individuals out of the nursery, into a world of collective traditions, and into an adult world of individual choice. Basically, it sucks when your concept of the world goes to pieces.

While growing up in the church, I was desensitized to God and took him for granted. At times, I considered him scary and hateful, not loving; vengeful; and boring, based on my truthful inner thoughts about God. Even though I would never openly say it, I thought it. How could I love a God who allowed children to go through suicides, physical and mental abuse and neglect, incest, sexual abuse, violence, pornography, abortions, drugs, and alcohol—so much pain and abuse and emotional agony? I was in hell! And I blamed him for every bad thing that happened in my childhood—incest; sexual molestation; physical, mental, and emotional abuse and neglect behind the guise of spiritual abuse from people who were supposed to love, protect, and guide me.

As a child, I was told in church that I was born in sin, that I had a sinful nature, and that I deserved everything that happened to me. I was told not to pray for myself but for others. These were my inner thoughts about myself—my inner critical parent speaking: I saw myself as a powerless victim to all the world. The world was a big toilet, and I was the biggest turd in it.

I am a firm believer that true learning comes from being outside. When I hear people talk about identity being tied to a place and the outdoor landscape of their childhood, I am transported back to the place of my childhood. I lived in a city, but behind our small rented house was a three-acre fruit orchard. That was a haven for me, my seven siblings, and childhood friends. We went there to heal after consistent bouts of physically abuse from my single-parent mother, who, according to our court-ordered social worker, was a textbook child abuser and batterer.

The orchard was a magical place, where fairies and other magical creatures lived. There, we felt safe from the world of uncaring adults, who never ventured into our domain. I would like to believe that the owner, who remained anonymous, knew instinctively that the children would need the orchard for shelter and strength.

As I think back about that healing place, I realize that I learned a lot about myself and the world around me. Where violence and heroism merged, I learned not only to climb trees, but I chose to climb the biggest trees and reach for the highest fruits, which always tasted better than the rest. There, I learned about virtues, like truthfulness, discernment, tact, forgiveness, justice, compassion, assertiveness, and—most of all—honor among men and women, just by playing cowboys and Indians, hide-and-seek, and war and peace (a free-play concept). These virtues became important to me as I grew into adulthood because I was able to feel safe enough to learn and reflect upon the duality of suffering and nightmares in my home, living with my mother, versus the peace and safety of the orchard, just outside my back door. This boundary allowed me to temporarily escape the shame, guilt, fear, and humiliation of multigenerational abuse within my home situation.

The poet Ralph Waldo Emerson couldn't have said it better than what he wrote about nature:

> Standing on the bare ground, my head bathed by the blithe air and uplifted into infinite space, all mean egotism vanishes, I become a transparent eyeball, I am nothing. I see all the currents of the Universal Being circulate through me—I am part or particle of God.

I have learned that just like our imaginations organize our brains, language also organizes our brains—a cognitive map, of sorts. I realized how being a part of a place and growing up in a place can also be tied to people with multigenerational abuse experiences and backgrounds. Blindly walking around like zombies, unable to connect the dots, acting out self-destructively, like a truck driving downhill without brakes, unaware of its devastating impact on our future generations—this inferno time bomb ticking in our heads.

I hear people talk about how one's identity can be tied to a place of harm or healing, if abused as children. These abused children are infused and hardwired with strong survival instincts in place. As they grow into adulthood, those untreated hardwired survival skills are seen as inappropriate and problematic in all aspects of their lives and lifestyles. Those untreated patterns that go back to memories of childhood landscapes and abuse are passed down from generation to generation.

I understand and believe that true learning and healing comes from being outside, in nature, whenever possible, culturally communing with and "Edenistically" close to nature, with a group of loving and supportive family or friends of choice. This will assist in the healing process and bring about a harmonious balance in healing work, versus imbalance between the emotional and mental maturation process when it comes to prevention for at-risk youth and intervention for adults.

Mother Mary and Me

Jesus, with whom I've had up-close-and-personal experiences and a relationship since I was a child, met the beautiful angel of death, the archangel Michael. I had conversations with God, all because I called on Jesus as a child. God directed my footsteps. My ego felt smug.

The following is a synopsis of what occurred with the contact I had with mother Mary. I was about fifty-four years old when mother Mary came to me at three separate times within four months. The first two times that she appeared to me, I cussed her out and told her how I felt about her and her religion. I told her to leave me the hell alone because I wasn't Catholic, and I said all these things before she could get a word out. I told her, I didn't believe in her and some other "really not nice things, like, "What is the deal with the dead babies found buried underneath the ground in the nunneries." Why was that happening?

The second time she visited me, I called her the whore of Babylon. And I said some things about her not protecting her children from harm. What kind of mother/ queen of heaven allows children, single parents, and the elderly to be the spoils of this man's world?

She never said a word; she actively listened to my scorching tirade about her and her so-called religion, which had all the riches in the world and how they obtained those riches in her name. She immediately left after each of my lengthy bitch sessions, as I told her, "Bugger off, and don't come back." In my mind, I was justifiably angry, which is my go-to place when I am deeply hurt, pissed, or scared. At those times, I was super-pissed, and that was the dish I was serving her.

The third time she visited me, I was incensed that she had dared to show up again. I thought, *She is a glutton for punishment. Didn't her entourage of angelic beings warn her to leave me alone because I have a big gun for her and her religion, and I have a lot of bullets in it?*

Before I could get a word out of my mouth, she said, "Lou, Lou, what you have seen and what you have heard was not me. It's what man has made me. This is who I am, and I want to work with you."

It took me about three seconds to ponder what she had said and to realize that for most of my life, I too had been painfully misunderstood. I said, "Okay, we can work, then."

Then she left. She's a lady of few words, but boy, are they powerful! During this whole process, she healed me of my serious, deep-seated mother issues and covered me with mercy over my shame and grief over my abortions as a young woman. I am assuming that's why mother Mary showed up—because I was open and willing to talk to Kuan Yin, who is the Asian version of mother Mary. Talk about remembering when and eating humble pie. I've shared the story with very few people, and one was a Catholic priest. When I shared the story with him, he kept crossing himself—I think he crossed himself about twenty times.

The other part of this irony is that when I go into my dream time, I report to a female deity, and I believe it's her, so she's my boss.

The Sacred Heart of the Holy Mother

A lot of Americans have had to lose some of their indigenous beliefs, traditions, and cultural norms as a result of basic survival adaptations. So did the holy mother, so she can relate.

Before the appearance of mother Mary, I had been looking at Kuan Yin to worship. I had put a statue of Kuan Yin in my yard. I did not realize that mother Mary is known by many names and has been given many names in many different cultures. I had read this, but it was in a different book of fiction, *The Red Tent,* based upon the book of Genesis, a thought-provoking book. I was very skeptical about the implication that mother Mary had many names; some of those names were demonized throughout the Bible, but my mind was open to the possibilities. The book of Nephi, chapter 11: "An Angel showed him a vision of the Virgin Mary in Nazareth, and the mission and life of her son Jesus."

Brigham Young University professor Daniel Peterson comments that Nephi knew that the tree of life represented the Canaanites' goddess Asherah, the mother of the gods, whose symbol is a tree trunk or a grove of trees.

Nephi makes the connection between Asherah and mother Mary. As he recounts his vision, Nephi calls Mary "the mother of God." Peter comments that this is similar to the vision Saint Paul describes in 2 Corinthians 12:1–4, where Mary arrives in "great glory," in her rightful place as divine mother, accompanied by angels singing her praises.

The fourth-century Gnostic text "The Apocalypse of Paul" describes Paul's being shown a tree amid paradise called the tree of life. As he is looking at the tree, he sees "a virgin coming from afar two hundred angels before her saying hymns." Seeing this, he asks, "Who is she who comes in great glory?" He is told this is "Mary the Virgin, the Mother of the Lord" (46). In 2 Chronicles 15:16,

> He also removed Maacah, the mother of King Asa, from the position of queen mother, because she had made a horrid image as an Asherah, and Asa cut down her or an image, crushed it and burned it at the Brook Kidron.

The Popes' titles for Mary were as follows: Pope Leo XIII called her our Lady of the Light, a safe harbor of travelers, and mother of the church. In the litany of the Blessed Virgin, Pope Sixtus V gave mother Mary titles such as Queen Assumed into Heaven, Queen of Peace, and queen of all saints, patriarchs, angels, prophets, apostles, and martyrs. Church leaders began calling her Mary, Queen of Heaven in the sixth century. In 1954, Pope Pius XI, known as the most Marian pope in church history, made Queen of Heaven her official title.

Even in 2012, Pope Benedict XVI described mother Mary as watching over her children, who look to her for maternal protection and heavenly assistance. Over the centuries, many millions have been taught to pray to mother Mary for help when they are lost, very alone, or seeking wisdom, in the same way they have been taught to be with the Holy Spirit as their help and guide.

The Holy Spirit as She—Hidden History

It was known to Jesus and his followers that mother Mary was the divine mother, the Holy Spirit. How were these teachings lost to the world?

Elaine Pagels, a professor of religion at Princeton University and an expert on Gnostic writings, describes how the early founders of the established church removed all references to the divine feminine from church teachings and removed women from any involvement in church order and ritual—a complete turnaround from how the Christian movement began. Though it violated Hebrew tradition, Jesus spoke openly with women on the streets. He treated them as equals in his teachings and in the temple and by including women in his group. From the year 200 CE onward, Pagels tells us, there is no evidence that women were in prophetic, priestly, and episcopal roles among orthodox churches.

Early Christians did follow Jesus's example and allowed women in leadership roles in the very early church. While women were allowed a practical role at first, the feminine was denied a divine role.

Pagels writes that the orthodox churchmen decided that "the teachings on the Divine Mother and the feminine principle are not the true teachings of Jesus Christ." They, therefore, were not included in the canon of scripture that became the New Testament in the early third century.

Author Rosemary Radford Ruether describes the idea of a feminine Holy Spirit as too much a female deity for patriarchal Christian orthodoxy. Reuther is an American feminist scholar and Catholic theologian and an advocate of women's ordination.

> Come hidden Mother; come thou art manifest in thy deeds.
> Holy Dove that bearest the twin young; come, hidden mother; come, thou that art manifest in thy deeds Come and partake with us in this Eucharist which we celebrate in thy name, and in the love-feast in which we are gathered together at thy call. (Acts of Thomas 5:50)

In their book *Mary Magdalene and the Divine Feminine: Jesus' Lost Teaching on Woman,* Annice Booth and Elizabeth Clare Prophet looked at the meaning of another title the church gave mother Mary in the 1960s, after the first moon landing: mother of the universe. Most etymologists agree that the word *matter* (created substance) is derived from the Latin word *mater,* which is mother. This is not an accident. The divine mother is creator of all matter, the divine birther of all that is. Many indigenous peoples around the world referred to the divine as Mother Earth and Father Sky. They know that both masculine and feminine energies are required for creating; this was also understood by the early Christians.

The Gnostics were an early Christians sect. They did not believe at the vengeful, angry God of the Old Testament was the true God and named him the *Demiurge*. In Gnosticism and other theological systems, a demiurge is a heavenly being, subordinate to the supreme being that is considered to be the comptroller of the material world and antagonistic to all that is purely spiritual (*Oxford Dictionary*). The Gnostic gospel of Thomas quotes Jesus as saying that there is no need for a human intermediary or earthly hierarchy—we can come to know God on our own. They also place mother Mary as divine mother at the heart of their teaching.

The Roman emperor Constantine decreed Christianity as the official religion of Rome in 1313 CE. During that era, the theologian Quintus Septimius Florens Tertullianus, an early Christian author from Carthage, wrote that women were the "devil's gateway." He blamed humankind's separation from God on women, claiming, "You are the unsealer of that (forbidden) tree; you are the first deserter of the divine law: you are she who persuaded him whom the devil was not valiant enough to attack."

He goes on to credit women with having "destroyed so easily God's image" and blames them for the crucifixion of Jesus.

The church upheld Tertullian's teachings, and the concept of the divine feminine was forbidden in mainstream Christian teachings. However, the Gnostic teachings continued; they were labeled heretics. The church became part of the Roman city-state, creating official canons and creeds that were enforced with political and military force.

Malakai described that religious and governmental heads were "the same." The church began to actively suppress and try to destroy Gnostic writings and teachings ("Pandora's Box," written by Hesiod, a Greek poet who lived about 700 BCE).

In 1945, the truth reappeared.

Ancient manuscripts were discovered near Nag Hammadi, Egypt. Thirteen papyrus volumes revealed fifty-two early Gnostic Christian writings. Mostly written during the third and fourth centuries, they offered a view of life and the teachings of Jesus that was different from that which the church had offered humankind since the third century. Because they are Gnostic writings, the Nag Hammadi text also speaks of a God who is divine mother as well as divine Father. In the book *The Gnostic Gospels*, Elaine Pagels writes that Gnostic writings depicted God as mother in three distinct ways: as part of an original couple; as the Holy Spirit or third person of the Trinity; and as wisdom. Due to the suppression of the truth of mother Mary's identity, the idea that God could be both father and mother is still unacceptable to millions.

The early church fathers removed or changed many of these references. The text also was intentionally made more masculine during the centuries before the printing press, when monks and scribes interpreted, translated, and copied the scriptures by hand, church orthodoxy, and the divine feminine.

In September 2012, the world media reported on the discovery of a fragment of a Coptic papyrus that contained the quote: "Jesus said to them, My wife ... she will be able to be my disciple." Elaine Pagels commented on this discovery in an interview on National Public Radio. Professor Pagels noted that of the more than fifty texts, many of these were "secret gospels" that only were published within the last few decades, including the Gnostic gospel of Thomas, in which Jesus speaks of "my mother, the Holy Spirit."

This gospel was widely read until it was left out of the official canon. Jesus and his teachings were considered a dangerous threat by the church, which permitted only one official set of beliefs. Constantine and his bishops created a canon of what they said were authorized teachings. The rest were called heretical. The Gnostic gospels of Mary, Philip, Judas, and Thomas, which all speak of a Mother God and a Father God, all were excluded from the canon. The church orthodoxy sought to control how people related to God, to one another, and to outer authority. The Gnostic teachings taught independence from any hierarchy. Father/Mother God is similar to the Eastern view of yin and yang. They reasoned that God also must be both male and female. One of the divine mother's earthly incarnations was as the Chinese goddess of mercy and compassion, Quan Yin or Kwan Yin, who is honored in different forms throughout Asia.

In representing the balance between the divine feminine and the divine masculine in Eastern thought and belief, the only equivalent for this belief was the Gnostics, Hinduism, and the divine feminine. Hinduism expert and author David Frawley sees the Gnostic concept of Father/Mother God as similar to the Hindu teaching of a divine male and divine female, represented by a Hindu god and his shakti (wife or consort), who is a creative force in the universe. One-thousand-year-old stone sculpted on Elephanta Island in India portrays the figure of the Hindu god Shiva as a male on one side and female on the other. It is known as *Ardhanarishvara*, the lord who is both male and female, an interesting note that seems to connect the dots for me and has stayed in my mind forever.

A human fetus does not develop its external sexual organs until seven weeks after fertilization; the fetus appears to be sexually indifferent, looking neither male nor female. Over the next five weeks, the fetus begins producing hormones and the sex organs grow into either male or female organs (Wiki, "Sexual Differentiation in Humans").

The Bible, the Torah, and the Quran usually describe angels as being male with shining auras. However, a passage from the Torah in the Bible, Zechariah 5:9, describe separate genders of angels. Two female angels lift a basket, and a male angel answers the prophet Zechariah's question. Then I looked up and there before me were two women, with the wind in their wings they had wings like those of a stork. Angels have gender-specific energy that relates to the type of work they do on earth.

Doreen Virtue in the angel therapy handbook as celestial beings: They don't have genders. They have their specific fortes and characteristics give them the stick male and female energies and personas. Gender relates to the energy of their specialties. For example, archangel Michael's strong protectiveness is very male, but he looked androgynous to me. He had a strong masculine build, but his face had distinctive feminine features. It's hard to explain—like the features of drag queen RuPaul in men's clothes.

Where in the World Are Women Not Oppressed by Men?

WOMAN—*Wisdom Over Man and Nature* EVOW

Wisdom is referred to as *she*. In Proverbs 1:20–33; 8:1–9:12, wisdom is personified as a woman who has much to offer, including enduring wealth and prosperity and life to anyone who will heed her words (Proverbs 8:18, 35).

Who is a woman? When comparing God, man, and woman, we can see the correlation between God and woman. God gives life, takes life, forgives unconditionally, loves unconditionally. Woman gives life, can take life, forgives unconditionally, loves unconditionally. Man can't give life or take life; he doesn't forgive unconditionally or love unconditionally.

Woman is of a higher vibration, created from the love God had for man. She is complete love, taken from man and formed to perfection.

> On the sixth day, God placed man in a deep sleep formed woman; then presented her to man. God presented woman to man, as a gift. (Genesis 2:21)

GIFT—God Is Forever Timeless

Gift is the label God placed upon woman. The love of a woman is the gift and promise of God's eternal love to man.

AWAKEN—Allow Wisdom, Allow Knowledge, Evolve Now

Although man was created first, he was not the first to be awakened. There were two trees in the garden—the tree of eternal life and the tree of knowledge—"but of the tree of the knowledge of good and evil, thou shall not eat of it: for the day that thou eat thereof doubt you surely die" (Genesis 2:17).

God spoke to woman through the voice of man, who simply repeated God's word, devoid of thought. God told man what to say for woman to respond, according to his will. By learning God's Word to man, he gave birth to woman's mind, and she began to think. When woman's mind reached beyond man's ability to explain God's Word, she saw a greater understanding than that of man.

The Tree of Knowledge—Man's Awakening

When woman began to think for herself, she no longer relied on man's words or intercession. She saw the answers to her questions of a God she could not see, hear, feel, or touch. This yearning to know God enticed her to partake from the forbidden tree (Genesis 3:5). Woman then was awakened and able to see God for herself. She did not hide when God appeared to her for the first time because she had a greater understanding than that of man. God began to teach woman all that he had taught man and much more. When God spoke to woman, her thoughts evolved toward her true purpose in life, which is love.

BIRTH—Bring into Reality through Her

Woman was created to be the facilitator of life, as God in the flesh. She was given dominion over all as the mother of creation, with the ability to give birth and to love unconditionally. Woman possesses the attributes of God himself. The essence of a woman is life, which is love.

LIFE—Love Is Forever Eternal

Love is the highest vibration of creation. The voice of God-fearing man balances the vibration of woman, allowing her to gain clarity, understanding, and control over her emotions. The knowledge of women is God's ultimate test for men! When God instructed woman to awaken man, she gave birth to his thought in understanding; she must teach, guide, and protect his innocence from being led astray by his thoughts.

God never commanded woman not to eat from the tree of life or to feed any of it to man. Therefore, woman did not sin, according to God. According to man, however, woman committed the first sin, which humankind has been using as an excuse to oppress women.

My Religion Is Music

It's a bittersweet symphony, this life—trying to make ends meet, trying to find some money, and then you die. I never pray, but tonight, I'm on my knees. Change my heart, Lord. I can change. I can change. The Holy Spirit hears my heart moan.

In your life, you have these songs—songs of periods of your life that lift your vibration, affecting your heart, body, mind, and soul. These are God's creative moments, where you dance, paint, write, stamp—you understand. Zone out of toxic media, food, and people. He moved me from things that no longer served me and replaced it with nature, like the oceans, or the night skies, instead of nightclubs.

Grow close to nature, becoming more connected to the life of Christ. This is what God ordained for me, in collaboration with my walk with him. My personal experience as a world traveler, educator, decorated military veteran, and an African American female, my gender and my racial identity has been unfairly blamed throughout infamy. We have been targeted for all the brokenness of this world. We have been oppressed, lied to, lied about, and single-handedly blamed. The blame on women emanates from Eve seducing Adam to eat the forbidden fruit.

Mary

A tradition says that the mother of Mary was a princess named Gropte from Kharax, and her father was the cousin of his mother. He was named Nakeb. He was a prince of the province of Adiabene and a descendent of the ancient royal family of Medea. They became proselytes of Judaism, and because of their wealth and social position, they were very close to the ruling classes in Jerusalem. After they were converted, they were called Anna and Joachim.

Joachim lived with his wife for twenty years, and they had no children. This was the time of a great Feast of Dedication. Joachim took gifts to the temple to dedicate them and sacrifice them to God, but when he entered the temple, the high priest told him that he was not to bring any gift to the Almighty one because he was not blessed with children, and he was referred to as "a barren tree." He was informed that his offerings could never be acceptable to God, who had judged him unworthy to have children.

This was a great shame for Joachim. He took his gifts and, in great sorrow and pain, left the temple. He went home for three days, and he cried with his wife. A few days later, he decided to leave the village. Taking his flock, he went far away to the mountains, to live there with his sorrow. Eventually, he decided to fast for forty days and pray to the Lord. His wife came to the same decision. She shut herself in her house and began to fast and pray.

When Anna/Anne was sitting under a tree, she saw a little sparrow building a nest for the eggs it was to lay. She watched the sparrow busily engage in its work, and she sadly burst into tears, crying, "My Lord, you have given a nest to this little creature in which to lay its eggs and to have its offspring, but why have you forsaken me?" While in tears and sorrow, she felt a presence around her.

Looking up, she saw a flaming angel beside her, who said, "Very soon, your tears will be wiped away, and again joy will dwell in your heart. Your husband has decided to come back. Now get ready, and go and meet him at the big gate of the city. The same day, you are going to conceive and have a daughter." Anna did as the angel said. She waited for hours, but nobody appeared. At sunset, in tears, she decided to go home.

As Anna was going home, she felt two strong hands take hold of her shoulders, and a male voice said, "Anna, you were waiting for me. The angel of the Lord appeared to me in the mountains and told me to come back and meet you here. He said to me, 'Your prayers were heard, and your alms have ascended in the sight of God. You will give birth to a daughter, and you shall name her Mary. She shall, according to your vow, be devoted to the Lord from her infancy and be filled with the Holy Spirit from her mother's womb. She shall neither eat nor drink anything unclean, nor shall her conversation be among the common people but in the temple of the Lord.' We shall have a daughter, and she will be blessed above all the women of the world."

They were full of joyful certainty, and they knew that the divine promise was going to be fulfilled. When nine months had passed, Anne had a daughter as beautiful as the lilies of the fields, and she named her Mary. Tradition says Mary was the mother of all the world servers who came and dwelt in her and were born, nourished, loved, and cared for by her until they became conscious of their divine tasks.

The Golden Gate is in Jerusalem, called *Zion* by God. The Golden Gate of Mercy, the Big Gate, is where Anne met Joachim. The eastern gate of the temple compound is called Shushan Gate, which is presumed, due to a lack of archaeological proof.

The Hebrew name is *Sha'ar HaRachamin,* "Gate of Mercy." This eastern gate would be one of the oldest gates in Jerusalem city, according to Jewish tradition. The *shekinah* (divine presence) used to appear through the eastern gate and will appear again when the "Anointed One" (Messiah) comes (Ezekiel 44:1–3).

In Christian apocryphal text, this gate was the scene of the meeting between the parents of Mary after Saint Joseph's first dream, so that the gate became the symbol of the Immaculate Conception of Mary, as well as Joachim and Anne's meeting at the Golden Gate. It became a standard subject in cycles depicting the life of the Virgin.

It is also said that Jesus, riding on a donkey, passed through this gate on Palm Sunday, in fulfillment of the Jewish prophecy concerning the Messiah. The synoptic gospels appear to support this belief by indicating that Jesus came down from the direction of the Mount of Olives and immediately arrived at the Temple Mount. The gospel of John alternatively suggests that the Pharisees were watching the arrival, possibly from the Temple Mount.

Some equate this gate with the beautiful gate mentioned in Acts 3. Other names for the Golden

Gate, in Arabic, are the Gate of Eternal Life, Gate of Mercy, and Gate of Repentance. Of the eastern gates of the Temple Mount, only two were used to offer access to the city from that side. It has been walled up since medieval times. The date of this construction is disputed, and no archaeological work is allowed at the gate now (Psalm 87).

When Mary was six months old, she stood and, one day, ran seven steps toward her mother's lap. When she was one year old, her father and mother took her to the temple, and the priests put their hands over her head and blessed her, with great admiration for her beauty, gentleness, and grace.

When Mary was three years old, her mother and father thought that they were too old to give her the proper spiritual care so they decided to dedicate her to the temple. They said, "If we wait any longer, she will grow, and it will be difficult to make her detach herself from us. If we have to force her to stay at the temple, she will miss us." So they took her to the temple in Jerusalem, and when she saw the clean marble steps, she ran up and entered the Temple by herself, and she embraced the high priest as though he were her father. When her mother and father came up to the hall of the priests, she danced with joy in front of them and made them sure that this was what she wanted. The parents returned home in great joy, having the conviction that they had played their role in our great drama to be unveiled.

In various traditions, Mary was called by different names, such as Mary, Mother of the World, Isis, Ishtar, Sophia, Kali, Lakshmi, and Dakar. She is known as the mother of ten thousand names, the mother of Buddha and Christ. The one mother of both Lords is not a symbol but a great manifestation of the feminine origin, which is revealed as the spiritual mother of Christ and Buddha.

A violent society produces violent families, just as family violence affects the wider community. A violent society reinforces and even creates a ripe climate for family violence (Baha'i International Community, "Creating Violence-Free Families").

Where Can Women and Children Go to Be Safely Protected from Men?

Let us join with all who are the victims of aggression, all who yearn for an end to conflict and contention, all whose devotion to principles of peace and the world order promote the ennobling purposes for which humanity was called into being by an all-loving Creator. Let men and women and youth and children everywhere recognize the eternal merit of this imperative action for all people, and let them lift their voices in willing assent. Let it be this generation that inaugurates this glorious stage in the evolution of social life on the planet. Therefore, the essential merit of spiritual principle is that it not only presents a perspective that harmonizes with that which is eminent in human nature, but it also induces an attitude, a dynamic, a wheel, and an aspiration that facilitates the discovery and implementation of practical measures ("The Peace Message" from Baha'i writings).

We inhabit a planet that is always at war, and the enemy of your soul never rests. But don't be afraid because he who is in you is greater than he who is in the world.

I have decided to follow Jesus. He has never left me or forsaken me. The cross is before me. The world is behind me. There's no turning back; there's no turning back.

Women and children have been deceived, discriminated against, and exploited. We have been made sacrificial lambs to a false god, Satan. According to the Bible, God won the battle in heaven between good and evil. The devil was and still is defeated. He and his watchers were banished under the earth and for seventy generations. They are called Gregori, with Prince Santana, who was once God's favorite angel, turned bad boy, Satan, who, with his crew, betrayed my God. And God kicked them out of his heaven and gave them dominion over the heavens and earth until judgment day. Hence, our patriarchal societies control this world, based on the domestic violence and control wheel (Duluth model power and control wheel, video of Ellen Pence, cocreator).

With age comes wisdom, and the invisible gears of God are made visible. We are in training to become over comers (Romans 8:37; Deuteronomy 31:6).

In my journey in this world, I've been gifted with glimpses of the future—to know what is man's love versus God's love, which is key. To keep it simple, death, hate, shame, guilt, fear, and all component emotions attached to these are from Satan. His goal is to make spiritual and religious people feel alone and unworthy of love, especially God's love. This is a major and effective tool that leads to martyrdom, depression, or self-pity. He and his underlings work hard to cloud our awareness of God's presence.

You can't fight the enemy on your own. He's been around for thousands of years. Satan understands human nature and its intricacies. His minions are spiritual, lethal assassins. They are trained to take you out. I believe that some, if not all, of this new technology is the new drug of choice. On a large scale, it complements Big Brother, especially now that we and our world community are aware of the negative impact of abusing and overdosing on drugs.

I believe this strategic form of propaganda or controlled domestication is to keep us addicted to any form of electronic technology. It prevents independent thinking. It also keeps us from going outside and exploring our natural world, getting close to each other and to nature, and communing with Gaia, a form of ancient healing that keeps us in balance with our world. It keeps us from being overstimulated with electronic technology. Lastly, it keeps us sane in an insane world in comparison, not unlike the movie *The Matrix*.

The key to overcoming demonic powers is not by engaging them but resisting their temptation by the power and the blood of Jesus Christ.

My God's agape love, peace, joy, protection, guidance, patience, and eternal life are his promises. Throughout my life's experiences, I've come to know and experience my God as one of the richest, most glorious, most loving creators, as well as best friend, confidant, doctor, lawyer, and mighty counselor, who never fails to keep his promises. He is trustworthy and lovingly faithful.

As a severely abused child who felt motherless and fatherless, he heard my cries and answered all my prayers. Even after I committed suicide three times, he kept sending me back here so I could share my story.

My God spoke the world into existence. He formed us in his image and gave us eternal souls. He created beauty in the world and throughout the universe. He is infinitely more brilliant than the greatest geniuses imaginable. He moves mountains and causes walls to fall. Strongholds break with his power. His wisdom is unsearchable. His unfailing love for us is so strong that he gave us free will. His Son, Jesus, sacrificed himself on the cross and absorbed all our guilt—past, present, and future. There is no condemnation for those who are in me (Romans 8:1–2)

This guilt-free status as a follower of Jesus Christ is a good reason to be joyful every day. This is not an invitation to dive into a sinful lifestyle. Instead, see it as an invitation to be curious, finding your true identity. Make every moment of your existence meaningful. Live jubilantly. God guards our hearts and minds. It is a collaboration between God and me. I have a voice, and he hears me. I revel in the glorious privilege of belonging to the Lord, my shepherd, forever. The law of the spirit of life has set us free. As a result of free will, we are our own best friends or worst enemies, by our choices. And yet you are still a beloved child of God (2 Corinthians 5:21; John 1:11–12).

Shift from a Sense of Entitlement to Radical Humility

Thankfulness is the best antidote to a sense of entitlement. One definition of *entitlement* is "the feeling or belief that you deserve to be given something." This poisonous attitude and the misconception that the world owes us something is an epidemic in the working world and is contrary to biblical teachings. Thankfulness is the opposite of a grateful attitude for what we already have. If God gave us what we deserved, our ultimate destination would be hell, with no hope of salvation.

Thinking that you deserve more than you currently have will make you miserable, but a grateful attitude will fill you with joy. Be thankful that God is rich in mercy. It is by grace that you have been saved (2 Thessalonians 3:6–10; Psalm 107:1; Hebrews 12:28).

In today's highly interdependent world, individuals and nations can no longer resolve many of their problems by themselves. We need one another. We must therefore develop a sense of universal responsibility. It is our collective and individual responsibility to protect and nurture the global family, to support its weaker members and to preserve and tend to the environment in which we all live.

—the Dalai Lama

Even the most unreligious of individuals are genetically bred to desire to worship something. It is now a scientific fact that transmission and reception of thought is possible. Simply put, whatever you think of is what you will attract. Whatever you perceive, you can achieve. Nothing can be thought of that has not been thought of before. That's right—planes, trains, automobiles, all of our so-called modern devices already existed in the time of Plato and Columbus. Look at the pyramids—they look like gigantic microchip boards all over the earth. I think the open-minded scientific world can appreciate what I am saying (G. W. Van Tassel, *The Council of Seven Lights*).

There were wars in heaven not unlike the ancient Hindu wars. The battles in the heavens described in the Hindu text were observed by human reports. They depict great heroes, demons, celestial weapons, beings, and the supernatural, not unlike the still-controversial, bizarre World War II Battle of Los Angeles in 1942.

O man, you have made laws to avoid using my laws. Confusion, chaos, and war are the results of man's ideas, opinions and assumptions. Light alone is the essence of truth. Truth alone is the essence of wisdom. Wisdom is the essence of knowledge; knowledge is the essence of life. Only through knowledge can man express wisdom in action. I have given man life that he might demonstrate my knowledge through action and wisdom. (author unknown)

We can create more light by understanding that we are sacred and that each human being on earth comes with a sacred purpose.

Thinking is not something one does. Thinking is the act of becoming aware of what already exists. One does not try to think to become aware. One only has to move one's thoughts in the same light; then the universal mind rushes in to fill the void. The ability to penetrate the mind requires practice. In practice, the act of awareness develops the ability to awaken the nearly dormant consciousness to thoughts existing throughout time.

My sister-in-law, an Alaskan native, who lives off the land, and a very spiritual shaman, was able to perform a native, nontraditional wedding ceremony that had not been performed in eighty years through the process of meditation, prayer, and fasting. The wedding was in Alaska and was conducted in such a nontraditional manner that it had never been seen before. My mother insisted upon seeing the license. We invited the ancestors, and two mating eagles were present and circled us all during the ceremony.

I had dreams about my soul mate five years before I met him. Even though he is my third husband (yes, ladies, I said third), I asked God to find me my soul mate/partner I was preordained to be with. I knew from birth, and I cannot logically explain it, but it was just a very sure inner knowing. I traveled the world, looking for him. We had decided to meet up in this realm and work together on an important mission.

When I got tired and disappointed, I went to God and asked him to give me my life partner. I did a formal contract with God, and he heard my cry and answered better than I ever could have imagined. My current husband—my soul mate—and I are not racially or culturally connected, but his father and I come from the same state. His sister and I have the same first and last names. She died two years before I met him.

During my dream time, I had an out-of-body experience, where I met her at a crossroad in another dimension. That was a monochromatic white atmosphere, not cloudy but clear white. I wasn't afraid, as I was very familiar with where she was and had an innate knowledge of the realm she was in. She told me she was working as a cook at a big white warehouse on top of the hill. And I looked up the hill, and there was a big white warehouse, a monochromatic white building, with blackout lines. I never met her and had never seen a picture of her, yet I was able to describe her to him and share that she was okay and happy. She wanted me to tell him that she loved him and was looking after him.

He had a lot of guilt where she was concerned, before her death. She wanted to meet her brother's soul mate—that was my impression. We have been together for twenty-two years; he is my third husband and my true soul mate. My birthday is on Christmas and his is on New Year's Eve. Two years before I met him, three different psychics told me about him and described him in incredible, accurate detail. These details matched my dreams of him, five years earlier. Wow!

I have discovered in my journey that this is one of the ways God works with me—through synchronization, most of the time, and connecting the dots. Synchronicity is meaningful coincidences, when two or more events correspond in a way that seems highly inconceivable and are unbelievably yet deeply important for the individual, as it relates to significant aspects of their lives in ways that feel unforgettably important. For example, numerous individuals have reported significant, strange, scary dreams that appear in times of stress, almost by some other consciousness.

Most of us experience coincidences all the time, but these kinds of coincidences happen in the form of déjà vu. These synchronizations seem to happen all at once. It feels like something is going on, something bigger and totally outside the realm of reality, as we have been conditioned to believe it.

Be curious about what you are afraid of.
Be curious of any attachment(s).
Then start letting it go.

I was born a Baptist, raised guilty, raised in a church home in the deep Midwest, and subjected to massive spiritual abuse, manipulation. I was made a spiritual scapegoat to a false god. I had real contempt for the God of my church homes. I was willing to join a black witches coven at age thirteen, topped off with successful suicide attempts that would not be my last. I didn't have faith in God, but he had faith in me and favored me.

Wait on the Lord: be of good courage, and
he shall strengthen thine heart: wait, I say
on the Lord. (Psalm 27:14; 139)

This Is My Story

We are a people full of opinions about things we know nothing about, just scared shitless of losing what we think we have—a future.

Reincarnation

Before being born, I remembered the crystal council. They were gigantic beings of crystals, seventeen feet tall, with rainbow lights radiating to and through them. There were about nine of them, and they had me in a circle. Our common language was musical notes that I understood. Music can connect with the mind, body, and spirit, all at once, more than verbal language, which is a primitive form of communication. I was a little-bitty thing but full of power, like the cartoon superhero Atom Ant, a powerful being full of power and light. They were doing a last-minute prebriefing before I went down the dark tube into the earthly realm. The crystal council still supports me, guides me, and sometimes warns me about some of the problems that I will have coming through to the earth at the time.

I didn't care to listen to them. All I wanted to do was to come down here on earth and do my Father's will. The crystal council love me deeply and would have gladly exchanged places with me. I love them, but I had a mission to complete. I was and still am honored to do this.

Prior Lives

I remember being a little white girl, five years old. I had long, dark, Shirley Temple curls down my back. I wore shiny black patent-leather shoes, with white socks that had white fringe around them, and a full, pretty white dress, with the hem above the knees. I was buried in those clothes. I don't know how I died.

I remember being a beautiful, white, female British aristocrat. My father was very rich. I was his only beloved, spoiled, self-centered, narcissistic daughter. I was severely entitled. I chose to live my life independently and traveled the world. I had about three children without marrying the fathers. My nannies took care of them. I traveled the world and left my kids with their nannies and my father. At age thirty-five, I died of syphilis or something similar. My dad was there when I died. I remember him crying over my deathbed. He traveled to America from England, away from home, away from my children, across the seas to say goodbye.

I recall being a short, rotund, middle-aged male, a Chinese silk merchant, who traveled the world selling his family's silks on one of those old 1800s ships you see in the bottles. I was about forty years old, about five feet four, and had a paunch belly. My favorite color was emerald-green silk. I wore a green silk vest and green silk whenever I could. That was my signature or my calling card. I considered myself a dandy of clothing and loved wearing bowler hats. I did not want to live in China. I traveled because I had an arranged marriage with a woman I did not love. She gave me a son. I did not love him either. So I traveled the world and never went back, as a screw-you to my parents and their heritage.

Another time, I was a young native warrior, about twenty years old. I wore buckskin boots up to my lower calves. I wore a square buckskin flap in front of my lower torso, with the ties exposed at the waistline. I had buckskin bands around both my arms. I was of a slender and muscular build. I had to be about five foot seven or eight. My head was shaved, except for the middle; there was a ponytail going all the way down my back, with a single eagle feather sticking out on the right side of my ponytail. My job—a warrior, scout, and fearless protector. My instincts were to fight and die for my people. It was the greatest honor. This was very strong in that reincarnation. I died as a warrior.

In another life, I was an Egyptian around the time of the building of the pyramids. I was a six-foot-two, muscular Ethiopian man. Being that I was in Egypt, I could say Egyptian man, but I wasn't; I was Ethiopian. I wore some kind of white, pyramidal, small diadem headgear, with a golden symbol in the front that identified me and my status as an architect. I stood in front of the pyramids, directing and telling people how to build. I was naked, except for a white, wraparound, above-the-knee short skirt with a golden waistband and golden sandals on my feet. I was holding a clay tablet with a wooden stylus. I believe I was writing something in a language I don't even understand, and in my mind's eye, there were numbers flowing into my mind, like a golden ticker tape. The numbers and equations were all golden. Complex mathematical equations flowed, and I understood what they meant. It was a different language from ancient knowledge.

In another reincarnation, I was standing in the middle-top level of a pyramid, being initiated into a secret sect. The men who initiated me knew how to get into the pyramid. I was inside of the pyramid, standing on a small, square, white-stone dais. Above me to the right above my head, near the tip of the pyramid, a strong moonbeam was shining directly down on me during this sacred initiation. I had on a white shirt—it looked Grecian, draped across one shoulder—with a short skirt above the knee. I was a very slender, five-foot-seven male between twenty and thirty years of age. I had dark-golden skin, and my hair was straight, cut short around my ears. I believe I was Egyptian.

This was a strange one, because it crosses into interstellar wormholes, alien worlds, and beings that belong to a scientific/spiritual/guardianship hierarchy, in which I am in a position of service. In another space and time, yet existing in the same space and time, I am consciously aware. During my dream time, I know that was real, and I did experience it. I wasn't alone; I was with a part of a team of seven, as part of an interstellar contracting crew, virtually a secret cell, based on a higher being/inter-dimensional sphere of being. I am a part of a big scientific experiment, in which body metamorphosis can occur, like the different forms that water can be used and manipulated—frozen, steam, freeze-dried, vapors, etc. So can the human body be manipulated with vibration and frequencies.

I strongly believe that my team and I were metamorphosed into see-through quart containers for long-distance space travel. We landed on an earth-like planet with earth-like beings. We temporarily implanted ourselves into a town, where we studied the inhabitants and took visual notes from our brains' memories. We were reanimated or re-liquified into a human state—I don't remember that part, but to my knowledge, it didn't hurt. We were programmed to perform certain functions in an almost dreamlike state, except we were very active during that time, using a different part of our brains—our uniquely different ability to compartmentalize, our file-folder, biological-computerized brains—which were contained in a very versatile earth vessel.

Bottom line: we were in a mall-like environment, mimicking the indigenous humanlike beings, sitting around a circular table, eating and drinking and observing. That is what really stands out in my mind. Also, during the flight in the containers, I remember trying to have a panic attack, not because I was uncomfortable but because my mind was experiencing the culture shock of space travel and adjusting mentally to my body metamorphosing to fit into a glasslike quart container.

I have had a lot of out-of-body experiences, or OBEs.

In my first OBE, I left my body during sleep. I felt I was an orb. I was light and airy, and I floated and went into another dimension. In this dimension were three thrones made of white stone, a shiny, pearlescent alabaster. The middle throne was higher than the thrones on the right and the left. Sitting on those thrones were three Caucasian men, with short, platinum-blond bobbed hair that framed their faces and clear blue eyes. They looked like brothers, not unlike Zeus, Hades, and Poseidon (but it could have easily been Satan, based on the description in the Bible). I don't know why I feel that was the former, but what happened next somewhat validated it. All three were having a very animated conversation, talking to each other, and then the gentleman on the left throne looked up saw me.

The next thing I knew, all three of them were looking dead at me. The guy in the middle stood up and pointed directly at me. Looking in my face, he said, "Go—now!" I flew back into my body like I was slammed back, like a door being slammed in my face.

In another OBE, I floated to the crystal city of lights, and that's all I'm going to say about that.

Lastly, I remember living inside the earth. I was a small male humanoid, not unlike the aboriginals in Australia. We all were no taller than four feet. My tribe lived inside the earth with beings who were seven to nine feet tall, very slender, and blue-eyed. They were platinum blonds with milky-white skin, not unlike the Pleiadeans, based up on the descriptions I have read. They wore shimmery, blue-metallic body suits that sometimes glowed in the dark or emanated a bluish-white glow. They had their children, and we had our children, but we all lived together inside the earth. The tall ones protected us from climatic upheavals on the surface of the earth. We lived together in harmony, and we trusted each other. I remember distinctly being told by the Pleiadean-like beings that it was okay to return to the surface of the earth. I remember climbing out of the earth on a ladder because it was safe to come out.

Historically speaking, most of the world religions believe in reincarnation. The Tibetans believe in rebirth and consider the body a vessel of consciousness. For Judaism, reincarnation is a fundamental belief. The Cabalists believe souls are given multiple chances to get life right in this dimension. Buddhists believe souls come back in several bodies to perform specific tasks. Philosophers of great renown, like Socrates, Plato, and Pythagoras, also believed in reincarnation.

The religion in which I was raised does not believe in reincarnation, even though Jesus assured his disciples three times that John the Baptist was the reincarnation of Elijah (Mark 9:3; Matthew 11:12–14; James 5:7), along with the following: John 9:12; 14:2; Luke 1:13, 17; Mark 9:13; Malachi 3:1; Hebrews 7:10; 11:13–16. Contrary to the facts, it is still seen and considered a form of heresy to talk about reincarnation with strict forms of covert and overt discipline.

Letting Go of Separateness

Man has created the institutions of marriage, religion, and government. Our institutions have drawn lines around the planet that create separation between people and nations, religions, and ethnicities. Think of the largest puzzle in the world with a vast number of small pieces—this is what our institutions have done. We have so many religions, so many sects that are constantly dividing and then dividing further. Buddhism and Christianity alone have created thousands of sects and lies among themselves. Hinduism and Islam also have drawn mini-lines among themselves. Most religions create divisions instead of creating unity, which is the ultimate goal for humans on planet earth.

The evolution of humankind is presently in its great destructive field, and that is good. It is not bad; it is good, for it is part of the evolution of the transmutation of humans, meaning that man is preparing to enter into the vibration of a new evolution—you call it a new world order. The universe is asking all humankind to let go of the memories that we carry now—these are belief structures that we carry now—so we can get to the purest form of energy once again. That's called destruction, meaning letting go, releasing, and allowing the new to emerge. Think of a seed that's placed in a ground. When that seed begins to burst, it must destruct what is encompassing it. Well, think of yourself as a seed in the ground, and you are bursting forth. You are sprouting. That which has encased you is now destroying itself so that the beautiful strength of you can come forward.

Those who watch their gardens grow after planting seeds understand that when the plant sprouts through the soil, something has been destroyed in the soil to let it pass through. The human race and the galaxy that we live within have been undergoing these cycles of destruction. We are ready to finish off that which has been so that we may come into the new beginning of the peaceful lights, of the radiant light bodies we have prayed for and desire to know (Kevin Peter Kelly and Marina Nikole Kelly, *The Holy Mother Mary Is God*).

A Consciousness of Oneness

Everything has a spirit in the consciousness. Native Americans have always known this, as evidenced in their traditions, their communion with the spirits of animals, plants, minerals, earth, sun, sky, and water, as well as with other human beings; everything on this earth is considered to have a spirit and a consciousness. It is all spirit, manifested into matter. Everything is made of energy or spirit. Spirit is the reality.

The Unconditional Love of the Holy Spirit or the Divine Mother

The Holy Spirit is pure peace, unconditional love, harmony, and intellect. She is also pure acceptance, stillness, and gentleness. Anything that you hear or read that paints a picture of God as a punishing God is not connected to the truth of our beautiful Holy Spirit, the divine mother. Humans have been taught, brainwashed, and persuaded to fear God and to feel guilty for their "sins," but that is not at all what the Holy Spirit would like us to think and feel. First, she has told us that we are all one with her, that we are all divine. Therefore, if we fear God, then we fear ourselves. Second, emotions such as fear and guilt are the opposite of the divine attributes of faith and unconditional love.

Divine laws that operate under the law of cause-and-effect, or karma, do exist. These are not punishments handed down by the divine. They are part of a grand design that many of us who are on a grand level help to create or cocreate. As angels of light and love, we all very much want to enter this world, this design of free will, where we forget who we are and then have to find our way back to the awareness of who we are. Do you know who you are?

Who Am I? We Are Angels in Human Form

You are an angel. Can you grasp that? Can you fully believe that you—not your body but you, as a consciousness—can never die? The consciousness of who you are is eternal. You have a higher awareness beyond what you now perceive. Much of your consciousness is hidden from you at this moment—hidden in your subconscious, your DNA, your RNA, your pineal gland, and the parts of the brain that you don't use. Your higher consciousness is hidden in what is called "junk DNA." It is also the energy system known as your chakras, in your connection to source, and in your blended consciousness, which includes the consciousness of all the ascended masters, archangels, angels, and the oneness of all.

Picture yourself as that angel. Picture yourself being excited now that you have the opportunity to walk the golden path. Picture yourself loving God, the source, and know that in angelic form, you are fully aware that you are 100 percent a part of the divine source. Know that you love the source of who you are, the source of everything, the great divine mother and Father. And nothing can take away the fact of who you are.

The only real opposition we face is whatever prevents us from knowing our true source. We are love and light, the light of the divine source, the secret fire, the source consciousness, divine love, divine harmony, and divine consciousness. We are all of that and a bag of chips. It is useless to put in the label of Antichrist on any one person or group. We all carry doubts and fears on one level or another, until we achieve Christian awareness. We can dissolve our fears, worries, doubts, and judgments—dissolve them into the little white lights of energy that they are—back into divine consciousness.

Here is my heart of worship. I give it to you, Father.

Releasing the Darker Aspect

> Men are disturbed not by things that happen, but by their opinion of the things that happen.—Epictetus

The preacher, priest, rabbi, church leadership, and most of our faith-based and orthodox religions today still freely utilize censorship—private and public. This attitude says, "Don't confuse me with the facts." I learned a lot as I moved a lot, growing up, and in each church home I was forced to attend, I had the same basic rules. Do not, under any circumstances, challenge God's anointed. If you do, you can expect the following: condemnation, isolation, shunning, and character assassination. Church vigilantism is highly effective. The primary reason is fear that individualized interpretations of the Bible could undermine the power of the church leaders' authority and potentially allow heresy and false teaching to lead people astray. That is their historical and rational interpretation of the situation.

I called it oppression, once I recognized my emotional, mental, and physical pain whenever I entered the house of God. To me, it was a house of pain, of sin, hostility, ignorance, and indifference. Every pain came from that house of pain for me. These religious practices seem to take precedent over God. This was one of the major aspects of my life experiences with various churches and the reason for turning my back on my family's idols. I came out of my family's version of God, which was used as a tool of control and harm. These old traditions were passed down from generation to generation.

I was stationed in Texas while in the military. I accidentally walked into a major power meeting, with all different religious leaders present. There seemed to be about thirty or more different religious representatives, based on the religious regalia that they were wearing. Initially, I thought, *Thank you, God. They are all here together to work on emergency flood plans, shelter for the homeless, or—I don't know—world peace?* That was not their plan or their purpose. My God showed me that it was secret meeting. I was in the doorway, with the door slightly closed. I was in uniform. I had to go to this church to pick up some paperwork, and for fifteen minutes, I waited, and I heard men's voices fading in and out—distinctly louder and then softly talking in the back—so I walked back there.

God's spirit just shut me up, and I just listened and watched what was going on. They were divvying up parts of Texas, discussing who would oversee which region so that they wouldn't have a conflict, money-wise. The overall look I got in glancing at every last one of those men's eyes was the look I got from my siblings and children after catching them stealing a cookie from the cookie jar. Once these animated men, who had been having heated discussions, saw me observing what were they were doing, they hustled me out of there. They didn't want anybody to know about it, and that's what bothered me. Right then and there, I was released of any guilt about joining churches, a validation made by my God. He didn't want me there either, and he showed me why.

My God Has My Back and Always Looks Out for Me

I felt that their religious rituals were bigger than their focus on God. Let's not forget the bottom line—money. I knew that was the tipping point for me. I had God's official stamp of approval. He verified that religion of any kind was not a good fit. It took me a while to catch on, as I was enjoying my righteous anger against the man and the church too much. I was accurately hearing the Holy Spirit guide and direct my life. Yay, God.

Not all God's anointed are in churches. Just like Jesus's disciples had many gifts of the spirit, not all of us are called to do the same mission. I can honestly say that I sinned more when I was in church than out, so, like an alcoholic on the sobriety wagon, I don't do people churches. God acknowledged my affliction and agreed with me not to join people churches. This is hard because when I do my testimony, I get bombarded and headhunted to join this and that religion. I can't and I won't because of the conditioning process, where we can't question leadership.

My God wants me to ask him questions—questions today's Man cannot or will not explain, mostly the former. That's why I don't go to man for spiritual food or advice; I go straight to God for all my needs. Man has failed me time and time again, but my God has never failed me and has never left me or forsaken me, even as a child of five. Jesus has always been there. Even though my God has never failed me, I have failed God so many times, played with his feelings and emotions, lied, cheated, and stolen. I blamed him for every free-will choice I made that didn't come out the way I wanted it to, even though I was going against God's will, knowing he always had better options available for me.

I chose to go in the opposite direction and suffered the consequences as a result. When I repented and asked God to forgive me, he turned those mistakes into beautiful teaching lessons and gifts to glorify him. He turned my ashes into something beautiful, as time went by.

I grew so thirsty for God's Word that no religion could satisfy that thirst.

My God told me to make him what I needed him to be so that I would know "I AM that I AM." My God loves skepticism, and he has permitted me to tell you the same. Make God what you need him to be so you will know him. The gauntlet has been thrown down. *Note*: make sure it is God and not Satan. You can make sure by calling on the power of the blood of Jesus when you start your journey and all during your field research. Believe me—my God will not mind. He loves us to be curious about him.

What Is the Triune God?

The Trinity, composed of Father, Son, and Holy Spirit, is a great gift to you; it is also a mystery far beyond your comprehension. This blessing of three persons in one greatly enriches your prayer life. You can pray to the Father in Jesus's name; you can also speak directly to me. And the Holy Spirit is continually available to help you with your prayers. Do not be perturbed by mysteries of the Godhead. Instead, respond to these wonders with joyous praise and adoration (John 12:44–45; 10:30; Hebrews 12:2; Psalm 150:6).

Who Is the Holy Spirit?

> Because through Christ Jesus the law of the Spirit of life set me free from the law of sin and death. (Romans 8:2)

The most neglected work of the Bible is the work or purpose of the Holy Spirit in our lives. The Holy Spirit's job is to interpret the Word of God in the Bible and expose the truth about God to his believers, as God would have us to know him personally and individually. This is not man's interpretation of God.

The Law of the Spirit of Life

The law of sin and death consists of our sinful natures interacting with the Law of Moses, such that we live in condemnation continually. There is another law, as Paul told the Jewish believers, that sets us free from the law of sin and death. Paul terms that law "the law of the Spirit of life." The law of the Spirit of life is the guidance of the Holy Spirit as he gives us the desire to live a holy life and gives us wisdom concerning how to overcome the world. He helps us overcome our bodily passions, self-will, and the power to choose holiness in place of spiritual uncleanness.

The sins that bind us produce a passion to perform those sinful acts. When we say the Spirit furnishes us with the power to choose holiness in place of spiritual uncleanness, we mean the Spirit overpowers the passion produced by our spiritual bondages (2 Timothy 3:16; Romans 5:1–21).

Holy Spirit, you're welcome in this place. I submit to your authority. God's Ruah, God's breath, the transformer.

When a person is saved, the Holy Spirit comes in to dwell within him or her, replacing the desires of the flesh that are living outside the will of God. The Holy Spirit transforms the person into a new creation in Christ.

The Spirit provides us with the desire, the wisdom, and the power that enables us to gain perfect victory over every sin that binds us (Galatians 1:16; John14:16; Zachariah 4:6).

The Holy Spirit is a person. He is the Spirit of truth, a teacher, a guide. God has called him into our lives to testify who Jesus is. He is the spiritual life force in our human bodies (John 14:16–17, 26; Zachariah 4:6; Colossians1:16). Every single believer has the Holy Spirit dwelling in his or her spiritual body. The Holy Spirit never talks about himself but about Jesus. He convicts us of our sins and guides us in all truth. He reminds us to glorify Jesus; by him, all things are created. This is my interpretation of the law of the Spirit of life and how the Holy Spirit sets us free from the law of sin and death.

What is the law of the Spirit of man? See Revelation 20:10; Genesis 3:1, 13; John 8:4; 1 Chronicles 21:1; Acts 5:3; Job 2:3; John 8:52.

> The fool says in his heart, there is no God.
> (Psalm 14:1 ESV)

I thought it interesting that religions do not believe in hell, even though all the ancient cultures believed and wrote about it, and scientists can prove that hell exists, according to the Bible—Exodus 20:4; Job 28:5; Philippians 2:10–11.

When our bodies go into the grave, the standard depth, whenever possible, is six feet, which is the number of man, the number six. There are three or four places that make up the underworld and beings that live in the underworld. The first place is called hell; in Greek, it was called Hades, Gehenna, and Sheol (Luke 16:19; Deuteronomy 32:22; Psalm 9:17; 55:15; Proverbs 15:24; Mark 9:44–48). This is where the wicked are supposed to end up. It is a place of fire in torment for unrepentant liars and deceivers and thieves (Matthew 23:33; Luke 12:5).

The Bible states that hell, underneath the earth, resided next to something called *the gap*, and next to the gap was Abraham's bosom, or Elysian Fields, where the saints in Christ stayed until the resurrection of Christ—their sins being remitted (to cancel or refrain from exacting or inflicting a debt or punishment). When Christ died on the cross and shed his blood, he went down into hell and had the keys to hell and death (Revelation 1:18). Jesus Christ freed his saints from Abraham's bosom under the earth and took them with him into heaven (Luke 23:45; Matthew 27:50–53). Jesus called his new home in heaven the third heaven or paradise (2 Corinthians 2:1; 5:6–8; 1 Corinthians 15:1–4). Hell took over the space of Abraham's bosom and expanded (Isaiah 5:14).

Tartarus: Prior to the flood of Noah, fallen angels mated with daughters of man and had giants, and the giants mated with men and animals, and they called themselves gods. If you look at the Greek mythology, it is highly possible that the following of the angels who called themselves gods were imprisoned in what is perceived in an annex of hell called, *Tartarus*. When Jesus died, he went to Tartarus and preached to the spirits (1 Peter 3:18–19; 2 Peter 2:4–5). They were chained in darkness, and these evil spirits or demons were the fruit of the fallen angels. They are perceived as the true representation of the Ancient Roman and Greek idols.

The Bottomless Pit: In Revelation 9:20, the Bible discuss the bottomless pit, where locusts will torment man for five months, without the seal of God. And it discusses the odd-looking creatures.

The Lake of Fire: The Bible talks about the first of the four fallen angels being put into the lake of fire with the devil. We know that the first angel's name was Apollyon or Abaddon and believe that he is in perdition (in Christian theology), a state of eternal punishment and damnation into which a sinful and unrepentant person passes after death, which is where Judas may reside. It is near the River Euphrates and where the giants were called Anak or Annikans (Revelation 9:11, 14, 20; Matthew 25:41; Isaiah 14:13–14, 16).

Satan Operates under the Law of Sin and Death

People under a despotic government are guided by the principle of fear, and those under a monarchical system of government are guided not by virtue but by honor. The desire to attain titles is one of the central ideas of the spirit of the laws that countries' governments correspond to their principles. One of the big lies that Satan has initiated with humans is that he lives and reigns underneath the earth. The truth is that he reigns in the air, the sky, and heavenly places in the universe. Satan rules all technologies and our airways, along with electronic emanations and sound frequencies that can control our emotions and make us sick. He keeps us focused on the technology, instead of looking up in the skies, because he doesn't want us to look up to the skies and see that he's there, controlling our world (Ephesians 2:2; 6:12; Revelation 12:7–12; Dead Sea Scrolls, book of Jude, book of Enoch, ancient story of the watchers, who mated with the daughter of man).

As a result, the Nephilim, abominations to God, were created (Genesis 6:1–4; Ezekiel 32:27). The Nephilim were great men of renown—Hercules, Jason and the Argonauts, Gilgamesh, and great creatures of strength. Then came the great flood, God's anger toward the abominations. Satan knows that he has been defeated and that his time here on earth is short, due to the fact that he and his crew of fallen angels will be thrown in Tartarus, the deepest abyss of Hades, in the lake of fire, with the wicked, to burn for eternity (2 Peter 2:4).

Satan is a master hunter; fear is the master spirit.

Satan is a demonic spirit, whose sole purpose is to stop us from fulfilling our destiny. Fear always comes against us when we are trying new things. There are other power tools that Satan uses to stop you in your tracks and try to make you go back where you came from: lies, doubt, deception, peer pressure, shame, guilt, and rejection. His bait is loss of a job, self-esteem, health, position, friends, family. When fear knocks at your door, send in faith. Satan wants to keep you from knowing who you are and to prevent forward progress. Since pride is such a deadly sin, the one that ultimately led to Satan's expulsion from heaven, being humble is a blessing.

A troublesome problem can become an idol in your mind. If you consistently think about something pleasant or unpleasant more than you think about God, you're practicing a subtle form of idolatry. It is wise to examine your thoughts. Most people view idols as things that bring pleasure, but a chronic difficulty can captivate your mind, taking over increasingly more of your mental activity. Becoming aware of this bondage is a huge step toward breaking free of it. When you find yourself dwelling on a persistent problem, bring it to Jesus, and confess the mental bondage you're experiencing. Request his help and his forgiveness, which he freely gives.

"I will help you take captive every thought to make it obedient to Me" (Acts 10:43 NCV; 2 Corinthians 10:5; Hebrews 3:1).

Another demonic tool he wields expertly is worry—a real thief in our lives. We worry about past, present, future, failure, criticism, exposure, and loss of self-esteem. You are not to take your career to heaven, nor will you need it. When you worry, you act like God doesn't exist. Worry is having faith in fear, instead of in God. Worry says that you don't believe God can take care of you. Worry sees the problems and doesn't see God.

Worry pollutes the thought streams that flow throughout your brain. The more you focus on your problem, the bigger it gets. What you feed is what you become (Josiah 1:9; Psalm 18:6; Isaiah 12:2; 45:2; Matthew 6; Colossians 1:16; Hosea 6:6; 1 Timothy 6). Don't let your mistakes in sin diminish your sense of worth. Remember that you have been declared not guilty forever!

There is no condemnation for those who are in me, who belong to me. You are precious to me, and I take delight in you, so refuse to condemn yourself. Your imperfect performance reminds you that you are human. It humbles you and helps you identify with flawed humanity. So thank me for the circumstances that have diminished your pride, and draw nearer to me. Receive my priceless, unfailing love in full measure (Romans 8:1; Zephaniah 3:17; Psalm 36:7).

Some of the other spiritual beings that Satan uses to keep humans ignorant are money, sex, and military power.

> God doesn't give fear but power, love, and a sound mind (Matthew 3:15; 4:4; 1 Corinthians 14:33; 10:13).

I am the word of life—eternal life. I have always existed; I am that which was from the beginning. Moreover, I am divine. As the apostle John wrote, "The Word was God." From the beginning of creation, words have been associated with life. Originally, the World was formless, empty, and dark. Then I said, "Let there be light," including all the plants and animals. Finally, I spoke humankind into being. The life I offer you is eternal. It begins when you trust me as your only Savior—but it never ends. You can enjoy immense freedom from knowing there is no condemnation for you. I have forever set you free from the law of sin and death. The best response to this glorious gift is grateful joy, delighting in the one who loves you perfectly and eternally. Remember that I am always near you, closer than the air you breathe, and there was light (Sarah Young, *Jesus Always*).

Made by God, Made for God, Made to Be Like Jesus

Jehovah Jirih—my provider; Jehovah Nisi—he reigns in victory; Jehovah Shalom—my Prince of Peace

This is love for God: to obey his commands. And his commands are not burdensome (1 John 5:1). If your earthly father is truly a father, as God is, he will command you to do only that which is possible for you to do. If you do not do it, claiming he is worthy and you are unworthy, he will wonder what is the matter with you. God *never* commands you to do something you cannot do with his help. You cannot throw up your hands and cry, "You are worthy, but I am unworthy. Therefore, I am not going to do what you have commanded." Don't let fear control you. God will lead you through fear (Psalm 32).

God is developing my character to become like Jesus Christ, God is interested in my character, not my comfort. God doesn't see us as we are but as we will become.

Your name is written on the palm of his right hand. Since God is the Word, Jesus is the Word made flesh, and the Holy Spirit empowers the beloved of Christ followers, you are infused with spiritual powers on a supernatural level. Health, healing, inexplicable joy (even in times of difficulty), peace, and protection are not only for you but for your entire tree—eternal life.

I could go on and on about the fringe benefits I have seen, including the mighty armies of the unseen Most

High God having ultimate guaranteed victory. Satan has already been defeated. You do the math.

> The idols of the heathen are silver and gold, the work of man's hand. They have mouths, but they speak not; eyes have they, but they see not; they have ears but they hear not; neither is there any breath in their mouths. They that make them are like them, so is everyone that trusted in them. (Psalm 135:15–18)

History attests to flaws in man's overall rationale, based upon the numerous deaths and man-made wars over religion. I believe wars are divisive tools of the enemy; by nature, they are in the form of one-upmanship, or "My God is bigger than your God." To me, it's a form of insanity, going around and around, doing the same thing, over and over, and expecting a different outcome. A lot of religious leaders play right into Satan's hand with this issue. If we deliberately keep on sinning after we have received the knowledge of the truth, no sacrifice for sins is left but only a fearful expectation of judgment and of raging fire that will consume the enemies of God (Hebrews 10:26–27).

The enemy doesn't have to lift a finger. I believe religion is its own worst enemy and can be its own best friend, if the chosen in God's leadership (you know who you are)

are convicted in their hearts today (1 John 4:1; 3:4; Mark 7:2–23).

"The end purpose of the law is not to abolish or restrain but to preserve and enlarge freedom." Argued that within the state of nature, all people enjoyed natural rights— rights that all people have because they are human (John Locke, Oct 6, 2013).

The law of the Spirit of life has set you free in Christ Jesus from the law of sin and death. The Holy Spirit will give you life that comes from Christ Jesus and will set you free from sin and death (Good News Translation).

Among these fundamental natural rights, John Locke said, are life, liberty, and property. Locke believed that the most basic human law of nature is the preservation of humankind. To serve that purpose, he reasoned, individuals have both a right and a duty to preserve their own lives.

Holy Spirit, we stand in awe of you, not by might or by power but by your Spirit, Lord. Send your Spirit; come and breathe on us.

You can't live a godly life. You can't serve the Lord adequately unless you understand how the Holy Spirit works. The Holy Spirit's primary focus, almost exclusively, is in spiritual regeneration—renewing and transforming human beings into the image of Christ. The Holy Spirit is a person who lives within the believers of Jesus Christ.

Another responsibility of the Holy Spirit is to interpret God's Word properly to his followers. The Holy Spirit is our reminder, our helper, our interpreter, our comforter, our teacher, our guide, our motivator, our transformer, and our protector. The Holy Spirit is God's Spirit, God's presence. I like to refer to him as God's breath, just like the wind and just like the air all around us. He is invisible, yet we can feel him; it's like a fire stuck deep in my bones. He is very powerful and sustains life in the New Testament era (John 16:8–11; Romans 8:1–27; 2 Corinthians 3:15–18; Ephesians 3:16–19).

The Holy Spirit has a specific job—reawakening and convicting us through his anointing, appointing, and empowering us with his Spirit. He will work with you, if you choose work with him.

By the breath of God, by the power of the blood of Jesus Christ, and in the name of Jesus Christ, I decree that all those reading this book will be open to God's promptings and remember that we are God's people; we are special and extraordinary. We are not average. We have been custom-made. We are one of a kind, and of all the things God has created, he is the proudest of us.

We are his masterpiece, his most prized possession. We will keep our heads held high, knowing that we are children of the Most High God, made in his very image.

This is my declaration: It ain't over until God says it over. Keep on fighting until the victory is won.

The Holy Spirit gives us gifts—special powers for our mission here. For example, the Bible tells us that Joseph was able to understand and interpret dreams. The artistic gifts of Bezalel, Oholiab, and their fellow workers were God-given wisdom, skills, and creative genius. The prophets of Jesus Christ were given the gifts to see what was happening in history from God's point of view. The problem was that although God created a good world, humans have given in to evil and have unleashed chaos into it and, through our injustice, have created a new type of disorder. The prophet said the Holy Spirit would come to transform the human heart and empower people to truly love God.

As a result, Jesus Christ and his baptism on the Jordan River allowed God's Holy Spirit to rest on Jesus like a dove, empowering Jesus to start the new creation. We see it happening, where Jesus heals or forgives the people of their sins, thereby creating life where there was once death.

The religious leaders of that time were jealous of Jesus and his powers, bestowed upon him by the Holy Spirit, and eventually had him killed. Here again, God's Holy Spirit is at work. The earliest disciples of Jesus, who saw him alive from the dead, said that it was God's energizing spirit (the Holy Spirit) that raised Jesus from the dead. This is the beginning of God's new creation through

Christ Jesus (Galatians 5:25; Daniel 1:17; Judges 3:9–10,19-20; 16:1, 7, 12–13; 1 Corinthians 12:28).

If diversity is a problem, then heaven is going to be a problem (Acts 10:34–35; Romans 2:9–1; 2 Peter 3:9; 1 Timothy 2:4). We need to lay down culture and pick up the kingdom. The sound of unity is all over the world.

Indeed, all of us who were baptized into the Messiah have closed ourselves with the Messiah because all of us are one in the Messiah, Jesus. A person is no longer Greek, a slave or a free person, a male or female (Galatians 3:27–28).

According to the apostle Peter,

> I see very clearly that God shows no favoritism. In every nation, He accepts those who fear him and do what is right. This is the message of good news for the people of Israel—that there is peace with God through Jesus Christ, who is Lord of all. (Acts 10:34–36)

"For the Lord, your God, is the God of gods and Lord of lords, A great God, a mighty and a terrible, which regarded not persons, nor take the reward:" (Deuteronomy 10:17). God, who shows no partiality and cannot be bribed.

"And said to the judges take heed what you do for the judge not for men but for the Lord who is with you in the judgment wear for now let the fear of the Lord be upon you take heed and do it for there is no iniquity with the Lord our God no respect are of persons nor taking of gifts."

In life, we show favoritism by the following: favoring the rich over the poor; treating others differently and misjudging them; favoring one race over another, one gender over another, a person's status at work or church or over someone else's, and Don't judge according to appearance, and repent of all partiality.

> If you fulfill *the* royal law according to the Scripture, "You shall love your neighbor as yourself," you do well; but if you show partiality, you commit sin, and are convicted by the law as transgressors. (James 2:8–9)

God does not show favoritism, nor does he want us to show favoritism. He says partiality is a sin.

Holy Spirit, you are welcome in this place. My mind, my heart, my soul, my body—I submit to your authority. I worship you because of who you are.

I declare that the creation of this spiritual brotherhood, kindled and established by the breath of the Holy Spirit, will unite nations and remove the cause of warfare and strife. He transforms humankind into one great family and establishes the foundation of the oneness of humanity. He promulgates the spirit of international agreement and ensures universal peace. Therefore, we must investigate the foundational reality of this heavenly fraternity. We must forsake all imitations and promote the reality of the divine teachings. Following these principles and actions and by the assistance of the Holy Spirit, both material and spiritual, happiness will become realized.

Until all nations and people become united by the balance of the Holy Spirit in this real fraternity and until national and international prejudices are effaced in the reality of the spiritual brotherhood, individuals will not attain true progress, prosperity, and lasting happiness. This is the century of new and universal nationhood.

Sciences have advanced. Industries have progressed. Politics have been reformed. Liberty has been proclaimed. Justice is awakening. This is the century of motion, divine stimulus, and accomplishment, and it's the century of human solidarity and altruistic service. This is the century of universal peace and the reality of the divine kingdom by the power of the blood of Jesus Christ and in the name of Jesus Christ. This is my declaration (Abdul-Baha, Baha'i World Faith, Abdul-Baha section, 224).

How Great Is Our God! But Who Is God?

God said, I am the Word of life—eternal life. I have always existed. I am that which was from the beginning. I am divine, holy, and sacred. I am love in its purest form.

God calls us out of the darkness and into the light. He gives us an ear to hear his voice so that we will know who he is when he calls us. His voice reminds us that we have been ordained for greatness and not for weakness.

God directs (Romans 8:38).

God is a great King above all gods (Psalm 95:3).

Some of the names of God are as follows:

- Elohim—the all-powerful one Creator
- Jehovah-Shammah—the Lord is there; the Lord, my companion
- Adonai—the Lord my great Lord
- El Elyon—the God Most High
- Yhwh—"I AM"; the one who is the self-existent one
- Jehovah-Rohi—the Lord is my shepherd
- Jehovah-Mekaddishkem—the Lord who sanctifies
- Jehovah-Tsidkenu—the Lord of righteousness
- El Roi—the God who sees me
- Jehovah-Nissi—the Lord is my banner
- El-Shaddai—the all-sufficient one; the God of the mountains; God Almighty
- Jehovah-Jireh—the Lord will provide
- Jehovah-Rapha—the Lord who heals
- Jehovah-Shalom—the Lord is peace
- Jehovah-Sabaoth—the Lord of hosts; the Lord of armies
- El Olam—the eternal God; the everlasting God
- El—the strong one

- El Elohe Yisrael—God; the God of Israel
- Immanuel—God with us; I AM
- Yah, or Jah—I AM; the one who is the self-existent one

I'm alone. I am God, and beside me, there is no other (John 16:7; Job 38)

What a mighty God we serve.

God told me that he is not religious, nor are his angelic messengers. He said that religion is a man-made tool, kinda like Gerber baby food—soft to the palate. Babies don't have teeth to chew solid food. God wants to give us teeth so that we can eat solid food, to fully digest God's Word/food. Yet a lot of religious leaders have not graduated from the Gerber's level and neither has their flock.

> No man can go beyond his experience level. No man's knowledge here can go beyond his experience. (John Locke)

> Trust in the Lord with all thy heart and lean not unto thy understanding in all ways acknowledge him and he shall direct thy path. (Proverbs 3:5–6)

There are seven spirits to God:

1. the spirit of the Lord
2. the spirit of wisdom

3. the spirit of understanding
4. the spirit of counsel
5. the spirit of power
6. the spirit of knowledge
7. the spirit of fear of the Lord

He pour His spirit upon his People. (Isaiah 11:2)

God doesn't want us limited in our search for him. He wants us to be curious, just like Curious George, the monkey in the famous children's books.

As the apostle John wrote, "The Word was God." This divine Word brings life to all who believe in me. From the beginning of creation, words have been associated with life (Proverbs 8:21). The earth was originally formless, empty, and dark. Then I "AM That I AM said, "Let there be light, and there was light. I spoke everything into existence, including all the plants and animals. Finally, I spoke mankind into being (1 John1:1–2; John 1:1; Genesis 1:1–3).

The Christian doctrine of the Trinity holds that God is not one God but three co-eternal, substantial persons, just like we have our bodies (flesh), and our minds (Godhead), and our spirits (quiet voice inside, or intuition). We recognize the similarities with God the Godhead in John 7, where he talked about the new birth of the triune God. God the Father establishes the city; God the Son, Jesus, is the mediator of the new birth of creation; and God the Spirit, the enactor, motivates us to make God's will happen. God is not an image; rather, he is a universal feeling, the truest expression of love.

Who Is Jesus?

For the life was made visible; we have seen it and testify to it and proclaim to you the eternal life that was with the Father and was made visible to us. What we have seen and heard, we proclaim now to you so that you too may have fellowship with us, for our fellowship is with the Father with his Son, Jesus Christ (1 John 1:2–3).

Jesus is the living Word of God made flesh.

He is our Savior, God, and he dwells among us.

Jesus was birthed by the holy mother Mary to come here and incarnate upon the earth, a being who would be an example for us, as someone who can achieve Christ-consciousness while living in earth life. Jesus was born the Christ baby. He was born with a fully activated pineal gland, with awareness of his Christ self. You and I were not. We must learn how to develop that higher consciousness because it does not come to us naturally. We can expand the Christ-consciousness, first by developing faith in the divine love by releasing worry, fear, and doubt. Keeping a heart of discernment—yes; doubt, worry and fear—no. An expanded awareness tells us when we are in the right action, on the right path.

The Essenes were an ancient Hebrew sect and community; Jesus was born and raised in that community. They had much in common with the early Gnostic Christians. They lived a life of extreme simplicity, living in community as one family and sharing all possessions. They took nothing with them when they traveled, as they would stay with other Essenes who provided all they needed—food, clothing, and shelter. They provided within their community so that Hebrew law would be followed on all levels of daily living.

In 1945, some workers in Egypt accidentally dug into an early Christian tomb. Inside, they found a large jar with thirteen leather-bound manuscripts that held forty-eight separate works. Practically all of the works were Gnostic, meaning they taught salvation through mystical knowledge, and one of these manuscripts contained the gospel of Thomas. In Gnosticism, people are believed to be souls in material bodies. Only through true knowledge can they ascend. According to this religion, Jesus is the redeemer who came to communicate that knowledge and to liberate man. He communicated this knowledge to selected disciples, one of them being Didymos Judas Thomas, who is rumored to be Jesus's twin brother. Due to both his names, Didymos and Thomas which means twins. (Dr Bart Ehrman, The Bart Ehrman Blog: The History & Literature of Early Christianity, September 3, 2018, Jesus' Twin Brother, Thomas. "The Gnostic belief system projected. (Christ The Avatar)And if these teachings had been placed in the modern Bible, the message might have been clearer and more focused on the power that is held within each person.

They believed in mercy, honesty, and purity of mind and heart. They were peacemakers and shunned the concept of war or weapons. They banned slavery among themselves. Brotherly love and service to others were central to how they lived their daily lives. They were also healers of both body and soul. They strove to heal and cast out evil spirits miraculously and to foresee events and to prophesy. Everyone in the Essenes community worked and lived at an equal social and spiritual level, without any hierarchy. Each day, they would draw lots to determine who would offer sacraments, read the sacred text, and prophesy or teach for that day.

This was the community in which Jesus (called Yeshua) was raised. He also stressed equality among people, performed miraculous healing, and prophesied. He raised the law of divine love above any earthly hierarchy and stressed the inherent equality among all people, including between men and women.

I love you, Jesus. I just want to tell you that I love you more than anything.

Jesus said, "The life I offer you is eternal." It begins when you trust me as your only Savior, but it never ends. You can enjoy immense freedom through knowing there is no condemnation for you. I have forever set you free from the law of sin and death (Romans 8:1–2; Psalm 18:19; John 8:34; Isaiah 61:10; Ephesians 5:8). But someone will say that Christ commanded us to be perfect. Yes, he did. He did not command us to be perfected but to be perfect. What does this mean? It means to do whatever God has told us to do. When the rich young ruler asked the Lord how he could be perfect, the Lord told him what to do to be perfect. The young man chose not to do what the Lord commanded. Yet it was something he could have done, with God's wisdom and strength.

Whoever believes in me does not believe in me only but the one who sent me. When you look at me, you see the one who sent me. I came into the world not only to be your Savior but also to help you see the Father more clearly. He and I always work in perfect unity. As I proclaimed when I was teaching in the temple in Jerusalem, "I and My Father are one." So when you strive to live close to me— fixing your eyes on me—you are by no means ignoring my Father (John 12:22; 10:30).

> Jesus answered, "If you want to be perfect, go, sell your possessions and give to the poor, and you will have treasure in heaven. Then come, follow me." (Matthew 19:21)

In religious and esoteric literature, the word *Christ* has five different meanings.

1. The inner Christ, the hope of glory, or the mystical Christ

   The inner Christ refers to the human soul, which is the hope of glory as it unfolds and blooms throughout the ages, using meditation service and sacrifice. The human soul, after initiation, achieves a glorious state of awareness and radiation and becomes a savior for the lives around him/her. This is what Christ meant when he said that we must "be perfect as our Father in heaven," who is glory itself.

2. The historical Christ

   The historical Christ lived and suffered as a man, strove to surpass human limitations, and entered into a higher level of evolution and was able to relate humanity to the Father's home. He set an example for us to follow.

3. The cosmic or mystic Christ

   The cosmic Christ is the soul of the universe; the link or the relation between matter and spirit; the redemptive energy, which leads the life, sleeping in matter, toward glorious heights of endless enfoldment. In religion, this is called the second person of the Trinity; the Son; the second logos; the love, who is the attractive, coherent force and consciousness who holds all things together and who drives all manifested life toward an eventual perfection, revealing the Father. Thus, the revelation of the Son of God and the liberation of the spirit from the limitation of matter and form is the goal. This is the cosmic plan—the macrocosm or the God in nature (Romans 8:18–30); the resurrection from among the dead or the liberation of man from life in the flesh; or three worlds of daily living—physical, emotional, and mental (Philippians 3:10–17; Ephesians 2:4–11). The ultimate goal is to bring to the surface of our lives the revelation of the glory of divinity, which are forms that nature hides, for earnest seekers, to unveil the light. It also is to reveal the Father (spirit) through the Son (soul) and express divinity through the medium of form (matter).

4. The Christ, the head of the hierarchy
   The head of the hierarchy, or the Christ, does not belong to any religion but to the whole of humanity, to all religions, because all religions are inspired by the same source,

from the hierarchy. No matter how they are distorted by human intervention, the light of the hierarchy shines in them as guidance toward beauty, goodness, and truth.

5. Another Christ
   In old literature, he is called the symbol of perfection, the archetypal man, the perfect image of God. In the Kabbalah, it is called "Adam Qadmon, the perfect model of all form and first terrestrial Adam." As such, he is the cosmic magnet, attracting the terrestrial Adam and transforming him into his likeness. In the New Testament, two Adams were mentioned: the first Adam, the Adam of dust; and the second Adam, the Christ, The New Adam the New Man, (Christ the avatar a sacrificial love, pages 46

"The two Adams made whole." *Atoms*—coincidence? I don't think so.

Ultimately, the first Adam, the average man, will develop gradually until the two Adams again become one, when the average man will reach the archetypal goal set for him for this cycle of evolution.

In Isaac Myers's *Qabbalah*, we read, "the Qabbalah name man as the purpose of creation and the first step is upper Adam or "Celestial Man" (Zohar III, 48a). In today's society we call it "Christ-consciousness," which in esoteric literature refers to awareness on the intuitional or Buddhic plane.

Light Bearers of the Ages and Their Cyclic Appearances (Comparative Religions)

Throughout the ages, all religions from different cultures in history have shared common themes that are repeated over and over again. Christianity is like Islam. They share similar views on judgment, heaven, hell, spirits, angels, and future resurrection. Jesus is acknowledged and respected by Muslims as a great prophet.

During my travels all over the world, I too saw similarities in the creation story in various religious, in mythology stories told by the elders, and in books I researched. Students of anthropology and religion will have no difficulty in tracing the path of evolution and the extension of the mystery schools throughout the world. And the following are several of those stories:

In the days of the prophet Elijah, there was a company of men who were called the "sons of the prophets." These men traveled throughout the world, ravaging the powers of darkness and wreaking havoc on evil kingdoms. They had no tolerance for the destructive behavior of wicked kings; rather, they turned many to righteousness. They raised the dead, healed the sick, parted rivers, destroyed false prophets, and saw revival spread throughout their land. They were feared by many and respected by all. They walked in great purity, and God was their friend (Kris Vallotton, *Developing a Supernatural Lifestyle*, 17).

The next story begins on the day when a man, for the first time, felt that the whole creation was the work of a great architect. That day, a window was opened toward the cosmos, toward the future possibilities, toward the future itself. These unfolding souls, as they progressed upon the path, felt not only the hand of a Creator, but they also saw order and harmony in the creation. They saw a unity in all creation that was not a machine but an organism, every part of which was a living part and had a special role to play in the totality of creation. They were called the Great Ones. They respected nature as a great mother and saw in every living form an unfolding plan. They loved all of Mother Nature's creations, including human beings, and sang great songs of gratitude to the great mother.

According to Malachi, the holy mother Mary is God. He has told us that the Holy Spirit incarnated as mother Mary, Quran Yin, Anu, and Isis and other goddesses and wants humanity to know that the Holy Spirit is very much a part of the human world. We are not alone. We have never been and never will be left alone. We all carry the capacity of her abilities, her love, her compassion, and her grace in her magic. We have the power of creation at our fingertips. We can and will create a divinely beautiful world of peace and love. We will have heaven on earth.

The Holy Spirit's job was to bring balance, guidance, and healing to places and times that were ravaged by wars in misguided aggressions. Goddess Anu, an ancient Celtic goddess, is known as the mother god, the ancestor of all gods. The people of her time knew she was the Holy Spirit. Isis was the wife of Osiris and the mother of Horus, who was worshiped in his time as Jesus is now. It is said that Horus was born of a virgin mother. There are many similarities between Horus, Jesus, and Buddha. There are many similarities between Mary and Isis, both direct incarnations of the Holy Spirit. It is believed that the Holy Spirit has incarnated more than just once—again, reincarnation themes. The holy mother Mary is God.

All the living forms ultimately were necessary to carry on the sacred purpose of the Creator. Ages came and ages passed, and these Great Ones (Gilgamesh) left their songs as guiding lights for humanity. Not unlike gospel hymns throughout the ages, they taught the love of goodness, the law of beauty, the law of truth, simplicity, and fearlessness. They taught us to abide in faith and hope and in love. They taught that faith was an innate, instinctual understanding of the beauty, goodness, and truth in all creation.

Hope was the response in man to the great magnet, which draws each spark back home. Love was the communion with the almighty presence in each living form. One of them was a fiery soul, who, for the first time in the history of the human race, entered into enlightenment. He stood in the presence of that mysterious being who is called the ancient of days, Melchizedek, the one initiator, or Sanat Kumara. According to the post-1900 publications on theosophy, Lord Sanat Kumara is an advanced being at the ninth level of initiation that is regarded as the "lord" or "regent" of earth and humanity. He is thought to be the head of the spiritual hierarchy of earth, who dwells in Shamballa.

Shamballa is a state of consciousness or a phase of sensitive awareness, wherein there is an acute and dynamic response to divine purpose. Shamballa focuses on the purpose and the will of God, as the hierarchy focuses on the love and wisdom of the deity and is the planetary head center, as the hierarchy is the planetary heart.

He intended to enter into closer communication with the mind behind the phenomenal universe. He passed through all human suffering, and as he pressed forward for more light, for more love, the heavy clouds of human ignorance broke their thunder on his body and heart—but he never gave up.

He was running his marathon race on the planet, and he decided never to stop at any cost but to press forward to the good. In the dark deserts of human consciousness, he's shown as a torch of fire. Because of his ages-long service and unceasing sacrifices, he became the senior member of the invisible temple, of the invisible church, to guide humanity from darkness to light. Age after age, he reappeared among men, giving the same teaching, opening the same way, and expressing the same beauty.

We are told that he is on the way back to the world of men, to renew in our hearts a greater hope, a greater faith, and a greater love (Torkom Saraydarian, *Christ—the Avatar of Sacrificial Love*).

The more I searched comparative religions, the more I found tons of stories of similarities. In the Bible and in other esoteric literature, these great beings are gods or sons of God. The Bible says the sons of God walk with the children of men and even married the daughters of men. Some of the names were Vyasa, Hermes, Hercules, Zoroaster, Confucius, Jesus, and Plato, just to name a few. As centuries passed, these great beings, with very advanced souls, were sent out. Most of those sent were from our humanity.

Wherever they went, they revealed the great teachings of the hierarchy, and they created great frictions, upheavals, revolutions, and wars. Most of these great beings were warriors and captains of armies in past incarnations, and some were high executives in government. Whenever light or power strikes someone, it causes friction, until that person can digest and assimilate it, or until he rejects it. If he rejects that light and that opportunity, he will have to wait for another cycle until a similar opportunity occurs. That is why Jesus said, "I came to bring the sword, not peace."

The great teachers wanted to shake the mass of humanity out of its lethargy to clean and awaken it. It is a process of purification—physically, emotionally, mentally—through suffering, by baptism, and through burning—the intense burning of aspiration. Because Jesus was the first great one to achieve mastership from the greater mysteries—his human origin; his power of illumination and achievement—he became a bridge between the great mystery and humanity and called himself, "the truth, the path and the life" (*Christ—the Avatar of Sacrificial Love*).

It is amazing that all the great ones who visited the earth gave the same message, according to the level of the people in the conditions of life. We see close similarities in the language of symbolism and in their major life events through which they passed, and even similarities in their births, struggles, services, deaths, and victories. In the history of the world religion, you can find the names of the great ones, and parts of their messages are scattered throughout the pages of tradition, from east to west, from north to south, in all ages.

Most of them were born at the winter solstice and of virgin mothers who were endowed with great virtue, wisdom, and power. Each time they appeared, they came to meet a human need. In the Bhagavad Gita (translated by H. Saraydarian, 4:7–8), we are told they appeared "whenever men become indifferent towards their duties and responsibilities, and whenever unrighteousness and disorder increase. ... to protect the virtuous, to destroy the wicked, and to reestablish the sense of duty and responsibility!"

In this world you will have trouble but take heart I have overcome the world. (John 16:33)

Our faith is based on our desire to do God's will, not on a hope to gain paradise, with its groves and founts (Rumi and E. H. Whinfield, *The Masnavi | Ma'Navi of Rumi*, volume 3).

Jesus said, "Man looks at the outward appearance, but I look at the heart. I am primarily interested in the condition of your heart, and I work to create beauty in it. It is vital to set aside time for nourishing your heart." Above all else guard your heart, for it is the wellspring of life. A wellspring is a source of abundant supply. Since you belong to me, my own life flows through you." However, to keep this life flowing" abundantly, you must protect your heart from evil influences and nourish it with Bible study and prayer. Aligning your priorities with my teachings can be very freeing. When you don't like the way things look in your world, close your eyes and gaze at who I am. Remember that I am Emmanuel—God with you (Sarah Young, *Jesus Always*).

The Apocrypha are hidden books of the Bible. The gospel of Thomas has a commentary on Jesus saves, as recorded by the apostle Thomas, by George Burke, Light of the Spirit Press, Cedar Crest, New Mexico. The discovery includes the gospel of Thomas, the gospel of Philip and the acts of Peter. None of this text was included in the Bible because the content didn't conform to Christian doctrine in that time. They are referred to as an Apocryphal. It had a tendency to concentrate on things that one doesn't read about in the Bible—that was the rationale at the time and still seems to exist today.

If God did not want these hidden books in the Bible exposed to man, they would have remained hidden or would not have been written. These books were omitted or rejected because of political power plays and disagreements among religious hierarchy—Catholic, Protestant, and Jewish Bibles (deuterocanonical books).

Early Christians paid by their blood for these writings. This sixteenth-century conspiracy was conducted by men in power at the time. That's why we call history, his story. I would encourage you to be curious and think for yourself. Don't trust me; do your research. The book of Enoch is a great start, as is the book of Jasper, the book of Jubilees, for truth seekers and personal investigators. I believe these hidden books were inspired by the Holy Spirit. So many questions that preachers, priests, and rabbis couldn't answer for me were provided by those hidden books. That is my story, and I'm sticking to it. I would encourage you to ask God to guide you in your search for your understanding, as he would have you understand him.

Seek God's truth, not man's truth. Just to keep it real, the people at the time put their lives on the line, as well as their families' lives. I don't believe their sacrifices were in vain. I don't believe in coincidences. Maybe God waited to expose these teachings in his perfect timing—now that we have the technology, knowledge, and spiritual maturity to understand and to impart these spiritual truths connected to us—through the Holy Spirit, telling and showing us who we are and our real history. Now we are ready to accept the truth.

Extraterrestrials, Leviathans, Giants, Spirits, Unicorns, Merpeople, and Resurrections, Hybrids of Heaven and Earth—Oh My!

Colossians1:16; Deuteronomy 5:19;17:3; Ephesians 2:19; 6:12; Exodus 12:49; 22:21; 23:9; Ezekiel 1:4, 6–7; Isaiah 27:1; 51:9–10; 13:5; 45:12; 60:8; Amos 9:2–3; Job 9–13; 1 Corinthians 15:14; Hebrews 13:2; Job 41; Psalm 29:6; 22:21; 74:13–23; 104:26–28; 89:15–12; Genesis 3:15, 6, 1–4; 1:26; 2:1; Hebrews 11:13; 13:2; Leviticus 24:22; Acts 19:35; Revelation 12:12; 13:1; 9:7–11, Genesis 5; 6:4; Job 38:4–7; 1:6–7; Psalm 65:5; 68:22; 89:5–11; Job 31–34

The gods of ancient times seem to have been aliens. I don't know if you remember the Great 2012 Doomsday scare. The world was going to end. The Mayans—Mesoamerica, in particular—and the Aztec people had so many gods in so many dealings and had four different gods for corn. They had four hundred celestial sky gods at night and four hundred sky gods during the day. In the Aztec, Mayan, and Mesoamerican cultures, this is repeated time after time in their storytelling.

If you look at their artwork, it seems like they're trying to describe something in their style that they can't quite understand but labored over, and put time into it. Some of the art appears to be feathered serpents, and some appears to be circuits. Other parts of their art show what appears to be tubes, and some art looks like what appears to be technology. A very well-defined and easy to identify common item, is the small purse, these people are carrying. People wear masks in their artwork, and it looks like a child kind of describing something that he doesn't understand completely.

For millennia, like many animals on our planet, something amazing suddenly happened after thousands of generations. Humankind settled down, and civilization emerged. Humanity was ordering its society, creating rules and regulations, and laws emerged as if from nowhere. Complex tools, literature, art, agriculture, transportation appeared as if by magic.

These are some other examples: the underwater cities in Antarctica—leaders of world are gathering there; pre-Adamite beings discovered; plus other creatures considered flash-frozen in one day. It was a part of the Hebrew writings that were hidden, and they went with Adam and Eve.

The 1973 aluminum wedge of a Moorish river in Romania; the Piri Reis map; Admiral Byrd; the inner earth; the Sabu disk, or Schist disk; the ancient vases found inside a 600-million-year-old rock; 1852 Dorchester Pot; the Ike Stone;, the Ulfberht, Viking swords; the Bi; jade disks.

In 1868, William Meister was searching for trilobite fossils in 500-million-year-old strata known as the Cambrian Wheeler Formation near Antelope Springs, Utah. After breaking open a slab, he discovered what looked like a human shoe print, with a trilobite under its heel.

The Nephilim Chronicles: Fallen Angels in the Ohio Valley by Fritz Zimmerman questions if a race of giant humans once roamed the biblical lands, Europe, and North America. The biblical stories of OG. Over three hundred historical accounts of giant human skeletons are presented for the first time. Massive human skeletal remains, burial-mound types, symbolism, etymology, numerology, and ceremonial centers.

In light of the allegations of the Smithsonian conspiracy and the six-fingered giants, historical newspapers with pictures, and numerous historical writings from sane and highly credible individuals, it is perceived and believed that the Smithsonian willingly was an accomplice to cover up the existence of giants, when world-famous explorers—Magellan, Coronado, de Soto, Sir Francis Drake, and Admiral Byrd—talked about meeting giants during their explorations. There is old film footage showing a Japanese giant marching in an early

1900s parade. Is the Smithsonian another Area 51? What are we hiding? And why?

The deities were aliens. The change in humanity was genetic. The knowledge was given to a chosen few by the ancient watchers over humankind. Either humankind evolved over a vast period, or there was genetic manipulation in which ancient man was chosen by a visiting alien race or races to be genetically modified and then given immense knowledge. They gave us knowledge, religion, and culture. It seems to be a mirror of their own mother culture. (*Alien Gods*, movie directed by Russ Sterling).

We are not alone on this planet. I knew about aliens as a child, and it was validated when I went into the military.

We were used as guinea pigs to see our reactions to the information about the others' existence, to experiment with us and other things. This could be misconstrued as mind-blowing. This is why our military personnel are flipping out because we know where all the dead bodies are. We signed up for it. But it appears the powers that be are trying to kill us, to shut us up about this.

Check out all the officers, astronauts, and professional subcontractors hired by military machines, who spoke out about these converted issues of the others—whistleblowers who disappeared or had strange or mysterious deaths shortly after exposing their truth. This is just the tip of the iceberg because they don't have the ways or the means to protect us. So if they can't dazzle us with brilliance, they baffle us with bullshit.

When I was thirteen and fourteen, my mom and siblings and I lived in an all-white community, and I used to babysit for the lady across the street. Her name was Constance, and her husband's name was Scotland. They had two rambunctious little boys. Her husband worked at the nearby prison. Connie thought she was the legendary Tammy Wynette, the singer, and when I'd go to babysit at her home, she would serenade me with country and western songs. I was a captive audience; it wasn't a bad trade-off. They would take me on mini-trips with them, and I got away from my mom and my siblings and got paid for it.

I didn't care that on these mini-outings, she'd act as if I was her hired black nanny to impress her husband's family and friends. She didn't have any friends that I knew of. She was a highly emotional person, and her husband spent most of the time placating her when he'd come home from working at the prison. Even though they lived across the street, I could hear her screaming and hollering at him when things didn't go the way she wanted. I rarely heard her talk to him in an inside voice. She had him cleaning the house, cooking, and everything else when he came home. It was the first time I realized that a man could be battered.

We came back from one of these mini-trips late at night, and the kids and I were sleeping in the back seat of the car. They drove a green Gremlin. This car had massive windows around the car, and I could see the sky—everything. All of a sudden, I heard Constance's voice rising into a screech. She was looking up and pointing out the window toward the sky. She screamed, "Look! There's a light following us!"

It was a huge white light, and it was getting bigger as it steadily came closer, following us. She started screaming to her husband drive faster, and he drove fast. He was scared. We were all scared. The next thing I knew, the car was parked, and we all sat there quietly, not saying anything. We were all awake and motionless, in a state of paralysis. Constance was calmly talking to Scotland. He started the car and drove us home.

I had another incident with alien beings when I was nine years old. I had a cat, a yellow tabby named George. He was my cat and my only friend. He liked me and slept with me in our tiny, three-bedroom house. George and I slept in the back storage room. I slept with a butcher knife because our back door had a flimsy lock and a very weak latch. One of the reasons that I slept in the back was due to a weird incident, which has stayed with me to this day. I was asleep with my siblings one night; we were all sleeping in a big bed, about seven kids in all. I woke up and saw a small gray alien. It was small enough to fit in the frame of the bedroom window, which was huge, and it looked right into the bedroom window of our next-door neighbor, whose farmhouse was within fifty yards of our window. The being looked like the character Stewie on the animated TV show *Family Guy.*

The alien, sitting inside the window frame, was watching us sleep. I woke up to go to the bathroom, and he saw me watching him. Then, all of a sudden, he started to shape shift right before my eyes, and he looked just like my cat, George. The red tabby stripes appeared across his face, and the eyes, a beautiful jewel-green, were spinning like a top. It caught and kept my attention, but his really thin body remained the same. It didn't change. He told me in my mind, *"I'm George. Don't worry. Don't panic. Go back to sleep."* And I did. After that, I moved out of that room and into the back storage room with my knife and my real cat, George.

Realm of Spirits

Right now, somewhere on earth, on every continent, people are actively, consciously venerating, petitioning, thanking, channeling, communicating with, interacting with, and/or pleading with spirits. What do they seek? Healing, protection, prosperity, happiness, power, direct contact with the sacred—people have been doing this futilely for a thousand years because there's nothing else for them to do with their time. Spirit veneration has survived and thrived, despite thousands of years of brutal opposition, because it produces joy, success, and positive results, a prime example, (Joan of Arc. currently requests for contact, personal encounters with spirits, and rituals honoring them are occurring right now in modern, highly populated, sophisticated cities, as well as out in the boondocks and everywhere in between.

What more could you want from spirits? Well, what would you like? What do you need? What is missing from your life? Desires may be material, emotional, or a cure for an element that defies conventional solutions. You may need protection from an abusive spouse, partner, or relative or from enemies, goals, eviction, bad influences, or even from yourself. You may need a miracle. You may seek comfort, vengeance, reconciliation, or justice. You may not want anything; maybe you just crave the company of spirits. To truly know whether or not spirits exist, here are the names of just a few: Astarte, Azazel, Baal, Asherah, and other spirits of the Bible; Merpeople from every corner of the earth; in East Africa, Zar; Irish Sidhe and Burmese Nats; in Japan, there are the Kami, Kappa, and oni; and the Pomba Giras from Brazil. Let's not forget the spirits of Vodou, Santeria, Umbanda, and Candomble.

Spirits are world travelers. They mingle among us everywhere. Spirits travel with people to new places, where other local spirits await. Those who venerate or work with spirits don't consider themselves "believers." They know their own experiences are valid and true. Others, having had no experience with spirits (or being able to recognize them), do not know this to be true and may assume and insist that what isn't true for them can't possibly be true for anyone else.

Is it possible that not everyone experiences the world in the same way? Not arguing tolerance may be the wisest course of action. To devotees, no explanation is necessary. For those inclined otherwise, no explanation may be sufficient. For those who are curious or on the fence, familiarize yourself with the rules and methods of spirit working, and find out for yourself, but please pray before you do anything in every instance in which you pursue spirits. Pray for protection by the blood of Jesus Christ, and ask God to be with you. That's my story, and I'm sticking to it.

Who is or what are spirits? Spirits are powerful, independent entities who resist human effort to define them. That's the absolute, simplest, and most basic definition. Spirits are ephemeral, volatile, and fluid; they can be hard to pin down. Spirits have specific names, personalities, and responsibilities, but sometimes, spirits masquerade as each other. Sometimes, one spirit answers to many names. Sometimes, the same name may be used by several spirits. Sometimes, several spirits share one image.

Spirits are among the universe's truly sacred mysteries. Spirits resist easy categorization. Spirits challenge standard, modern axioms of space, time, and reality. There are valid reasons why so many have a hard time accepting their existence. But those who have had direct experience with them can attest that they are genuinely here among us. Modern scientific methods require predictability, uniformity, standardization, and the ability to reproduce results on demand. The modern scientific method is a human construct, created by people to fulfill human needs, goals, or desires. The spirits don't play by those rules. Contrary to scientific method, spirits offer results as they please, when they choose.

If anything, we are their lab rats. Secret text, myths, and legends recount innumerable instances of spirits testing humans. The book of Job, the prophet Elijah, the myth of Santa Claus checking who's naughty and who's nice is a very vestigial memory of spirits testing humans on whether to dispense gifts for punishment. Spirits are living, intelligent, sentient, and willful. They live outside our imaginations. We didn't invent them or make them up, although we have certainly embellished and twisted many of their legends. Spirits are alive in their way. No existing word can adequately express how spirits are alive—the inadequacy of language, like undead or the living dead.

Spirits possess their kind of consistency. They are true to themselves. They possess their own rules. Generally, those rules have existed for hundreds, if not thousands, of years. Those spirits who are temperamental, prone to violence, perpetually grouchy, or pranksters make no pretense of being otherwise. Loki, Papa Legba, and

Mercury (Norse, West African, and Roman spirits, respectively) are unabashed tricksters. Kuan Yin, goddess of mercy, is forever patient and loving, but the sacred harlot, or one of the Holy Harlots, Pomba Gira (associated with vampires, women, sex workers, cross dressers, and transvestism) makes no such promises, Said to be the disembodied spirit of an unruly harlot a controversial figure in Brazil's religious history. The Baron Samedi, is one of the leaders loa of Haitian voodoo, (Master of the cemetery, and Spirits of Death). Genes, a category of Haitian Vodou spirit, or Spirit of the Dead. These spirit are reputed patient spirits of the dead, adore profanity and ribald humor.

Spirits are generally invisible, although many can make themselves selectively visible when they choose (Judika Illes, *Encyclopedia of Spirits: the Ultimate Guide to the Magic of Fairies, Genies, Demons, Ghosts, Gods & Goddesses*).

Burn like a fire, blow like the wind, come Holy Spirit, we welcome you in. In their hearts, humans plan their course, but the Lord establishes their steps (Proverbs 16:9).

I thirst and hunger after God's Word. Almost all of my "Why, God?" moments are gone. My God has given me back my identity and peace and rest for my soul that religion could not give. I am secure that God is on my side. As such, everything happening in our world today is happening in God's perfect timing. These calamities are based upon man's free-will choices, not God's will. We are to put all our trust into God's hands. After all, God is greater than our hearts, and he knows everything. But do not forget this one thing, dear friends: with the Lord, a day is like one thousand years, and one thousand years are like a day. The Lord is not slow in keeping his promise, as some understand as slowness. Instead, he is patient with you, not wanting anyone to perish but for everyone to come to repentance (2 Peter 3:8–9).

Sign of the Times: Psalm 11–12; 52–53

It was the best of times, it was the worst of times, it was the age of wisdom, it was the age of foolishness, it was the epoch of belief, it was the epoch of incredulity. (Charles Dickens, *A Tale of Two Cities*)

Harden not your heart, as in the provocation, and as in the day of temptation in the wilderness. (Psalm 95:8)

Memories have a way of hurting you far more than the experience. If you are aware, awakening, and awakened, you understand what I mean. It's all around us. Some of us choose to keep our heads buried in the sand, but those of us who are in tune with the world around us realize that an awakening is happening all over the world—a major spiritual revival/revolution. The United States is, slowly but surely, realizing that institutionalized violence, oppression, and rigidly maintained economic and social inequalities can simultaneously victimize men and turn them into perpetrators of violence against those even more helpless—their wives and children.

If it is possible, as far as it depends on you, live at peace with everyone. Someone will be determined to oppose you without the cause. In this case, Jesus doesn't hold you accountable for the conflict. More often, however, you have contributed something to the dissection. When this happens, repent of your part in the conflict and do whatever you can to restore a peaceful relationship. In either situation, forgive the person who offended you. You also may need to forgive yourself.

Beloved, be quick to listen, slow to speak, and slow to anger. Take time, not only to think through what you want to say but to listen to the other person. If you listen carefully and pause before responding, you will be much less likely to become angry. Whenever you have failed to live at peace with others, and you are at fault, do not despair. I paid the penalty for all your sins so you could have permanent peace with me (Romans 12:18; James 1:19; Romans 5:1).

While Here on Earth, Don't Be Surprised by the Many Loose Ends in Your Life

Loose ends will always be a part of your experience in this fallen world. When God created Adam and Eve, he placed them in a perfect environment: the garden of Eden. Since we are their descendants, our longing for perfection is natural. It is also supernatural. Because we are Jesus's followers, our ultimate destination is heaven—magnificent and glorious, beyond anything we can imagine!

Your longings will be completely satisfied there. Tell your troubles to Jesus in prayer, and let him help you with them. Then thank him for hearing and answering (he heard your prayers the first time). Instead of worrying, seek his guidance and will for you. Seek his presence with an attitude of gratitude of what you do have, and thank him for it, while continuing to thank him for answering your prayers (faith in action). As you do this these action steps, you engage in worshipping Jesus and participating in his glory (Genesis 2:15; Psalm 73:23–24; 29:2).

Being a multicultural African American, I was raised a strict Southern Baptist, where the Bible, God, and going to hell were used as a dominant tool to manipulate, control, and triangulate my family and the living-community rules where I grew up. If you drank, used drugs, and committed adultery as a black female, you were ostracized and called a loose woman, but this was okay if you were a black male.

This double standard is not unique and is still alive and well today. I call it the moral circle, or ignorance, which is the hardest disability to overcome—a systemic, multicultural domestication; indoctrination for me and my family; and how our patterns of thinking or feeling and how we acted, reacted, and viewed the world as a whole. Based on the cultural, racial, and religious social environment in which I grew up, the damaging belief systems, a collection of unhealthy life experiences and coping mechanisms, and the survival skills of my family members, I observed that a lot of them died horrible deaths before age sixty, including my daughter at the age of thirty-four. As a child, I realized that my family was severely broken. As a result, I decided this was not the kind of life I wanted.

Hence, I escaped into the military, seven days after my eighteenth birthday, along with a healthy dose of righteously justified hatred for most religions, especially the ones that prohibited questioning leadership's behaviors and actions. I call it accountability to the parishioners who are giving the church their hard-earned money. You know who you are.

> It is not what a woman feels.
> It is not what a woman thinks she feels.
> It is what a woman thinks! (Evow)

Growing up in the church, I was conditioned and trained to never question authority figures in my church or home—the mothers and older women of the church. The power behind most black churches, which have been conditioned to maintain the traditional status quo, was originally a survival tactic to keep our race and men safe from genocide from white America, as well as keeping us safe from the ugliness of our society toward people of color. This is another example of cultural domestication or spiritual conditioning, based on the power and control wheel of spiritual abuse.

"I am churched out." Stop killing the messengers; get the message. Please cease using my God's Bible to hide behind to sin.

Empirically speaking, I have found that to ask questions or to openly find conflict in what the preacher says, whether out of the context of the Bible or not, is considered a one-way ticket to a living hell; that is, if you choose to remain in that church home and are a glutton for punishment. This is especially true if you have a business in the community, which is additional leverage. As I was growing up, attendance at church was mandatory, three times weekly. I have been a part of and observed these conditioning processes. Based on my experiences while searching for a religion of choice or a designer religion that fit my busy lifestyle, a saint is just a sinner who fell down and then got up again.

Lord, you provide the fire. I'll provide the sacrifice. You provide the spirit, and I will open up and say, "Fill me up, Lord, fill me up."

The Earth is but one country and mankind is its citizens, and as foretold in all sacred scriptures of the past, now is the time for humanity to live in unity. Let your vision be world-embracing. (writer unknown)

During my travels all over the world, I have been to places in the South Pacific, Japan, Korea, Turkey, Greece, Hawaii, Malaysia, and Europe. I have had uncanny déjà vu of these places before physically going there. These places felt familiar, like I had lived there before, and that even the written and some of the verbal languages were familiar. Then there are places to which I had a natural revulsion, to which I will not go. I freak out every time I think about going to those places.

All my adult life, I have learned to take this gift in stride—that I am the right path, but I am scared and freaked out. All three of my husbands—two were military men and one a retired correctional officer—probably could speak to the other-worldly strangeness surrounding our relationships.

In childhood, I remember small snapshots, pictures of my life. I thought of them as dreams, realizing they were mini-movies of my life as a child. My first conscious recollection is riding on a bus with blacked-out windows, not knowing what was going on, but not caring where I was going. It was not unlike being totally and bodily in a sleeping paralysis—being aware but not plugged into something, similar to the movie *The Matrix.*

In another snapshot, I was being hung on something, like a meat assembly line, with thousands of people in a large dark cavern under the earth. The assembly line attached to the cavern ceiling and stretched miles and miles above the floor, hanging like dead pigs in a meat locker. We were all in a state of paralysis, hanging from tong-like hooks around our necks and attached to our ears. As I came through the inspection line, I was given a series of numbers and passed inspection. I heard the word, *okay.* These beings had been studying me and my ancestors for I don't know how long. They didn't think I would remember and would hide it in a dream state. I am not alone; some of us think of it as a dream, but the "awakened ones" know it was real.

My perception through my studies is that I was a walk-in. One snapshot I clearly remember was talking to an uncle's dog when I was four. I did not know regular people didn't talk to animals. I walked out onto my grandmother's front porch in Kansas City, early one quiet summer morning. Everyone in the house was still asleep.

I can still hear the echo of the screen door as it slammed shut. I walked onto the porch.

Butch, my uncle's yellow lab, was quietly standing like a sentinel on the front steps. Using all of his senses, he sniffed the air, alert, while his ears slowly swung back and forth like big satellite radar disks, as if in a meditative trance but totally in the present, aware of everything going on in our neighborhood.

Butch turned toward me and said, "Hello, little pup."

"What are you doing?" I asked.

And he said, "Standing guard, little pup, and keeping watch." He said this while sniffing. We were not speaking words but communicating words in picture form.

At age thirteen, I was sitting in front of the television, watching *Hawaii Five-0*. All of a sudden, just out of the air, I heard a strong male voice, right next to my right ear, say, "You are gonna live there one day." Then a picture flashed in my mind's eye—the back of me, standing next to a young man, and both of us had on blue uniforms.

We were standing in front of a judge—and that's exactly what happened. It was a snapshot of my first marriage. I lived in Hawaii. We were in our military uniforms (air force blues) and were married by a local judge. This kind of thing happens to me a lot. These are gifts of the spirit. My grandmother had it, and so did my great-grandmother. I am informed by the Holy Spirit that a lot of God's chosen have this gift, and they are afraid of it. They won't admit to it, and so their gift dies, or they are labeled or seen as crazy or called a witch, due to our societal conditioning. If we don't understand it, if it doesn't fit our image of normalcy, kill it.

> He dwells in the secret place of the most high shall abide under the shadow of the Almighty. I will say the Lord He is my refuge and my fortress, my God, in Him will I trust. (Psalm 91:2)

The cornerstone of the religion of God is the acquisition of the divine perfection and the sharing of his manifold bestowal. The essential purpose of faith and belief is to enable the inner being of man with the outpouring of grace from on high. If this is not attained, it is deprivation itself (Abdul-Baha, *The Divine Art of Living*).

Take Me to the King

My next memory was that of being in church, and the preacher was praying to God. I saw Jesus standing in the middle of the aisle, with a shining light surrounding him. The first time I saw a vision was when I was about five years old—born Baptist, raised guilty—while at our Southern Baptist church in my hometown of Kansas City, Missouri. The preacher was preaching, and most of the adults in my family's Southern Baptist congregation were full of the Holy Spirit—shouting, dancing in the aisles, and praising the Lord. Then, right in the middle of the shouting and preaching, there appeared a white man with brown eyes and shoulder-length brown hair, wearing an off-white rough-cotton nightshirt with tattered edges around his ankles, and a pale blue bathrobe. He didn't say anything; he just stood there with his palms open at his sides, facing me. I knew he was Jesus, based upon the pictures I'd seen in the Bibles and in my grandmother's house. I wasn't afraid because I thought everyone saw him too, and besides, he was the only white person in the church.

He never said a word; he just stood there while the preacher prayed. The church members were praising God and were full of the Holy Spirit. I remember going up to the altar and asking to get baptized, and the preacher asked me, "Baby, why do you want to be baptized?"

I said, "Because I want to go to heaven." I was a very quiet, serious child and fully committed to giving my life to Christ, as I understood it.

Shortly afterward, I was baptized. During the baptism, I was scared. I had seen a lot of adults being baptized in the churches' baptismal pools; ours was always underneath the choir stands. I had heard a lot of horror stories from my uncles and aunts, about how cold the water was and them feeling and seeing all kinds of things swimming in the water while being held, bent backward, and experiencing full-body dunking in the water—stories about not being able to breathe and them feeling like they were dying.

Maybe it was because the preacher would hold their noses. A lot of the black people that I knew didn't know how to swim, much less like taking baths. They did not understand why the preacher held their noses so they wouldn't drown.

However, being a child, I believed their baptismal stories, based upon viewing previous baptisms, where everyone in the church is conditioned to mandatory attendance after being baptized. The baptized would come up out of the water, fighting the preacher as he dunked them in the waist-deep, freezing water from the swimming pool underneath the choir stand. The stories seem highly credible when I think about those times. I think the water needed to be freezing to reenact a cold river like in the Bible with Jesus, when he was baptizing his followers; thus, the strange sightings while underwater. They looked scared and confused, while gasping for air, like fish out of water, fighting to hurriedly get out of the water.

I don't remember when I started to hear the elder's voice inside my head or when I saw strange white orbs floating around the house or the black shadow people that I saw out of the corners of my eyes. You are not crazy; yes, these are glimpses of parallel dimensions. I didn't know what they were, and I thought everyone saw them but just didn't talk about them. When I was little, we would sleep on the porch roof of my grandmother's house at night and look out at the stars. It was beautiful. I felt very connected to the stars. I felt that with the stars was where I truly belonged, and that was my real home; one day, I would return. I couldn't explain it but just knew it.

The first time I died, I was about twelve. My uncles were drug dealers, and I lived in an all-white town. My sister was being molested by my mother's live-in boyfriend by mutual agreement. I had walked in and caught them in the act. I blew the whistle, but my mother sided with her lover and my sister and said that I had lied; that it hadn't happened. I was told that I was a liar, and if I didn't shut up about it, I was going to be beaten to death by my mom.

I was shocked, scared, confused, and depressed (stuffed anger). My extended family believed me but wouldn't confront my mother or go to the police to turn them in. Who was going to be responsible for eight kids? If welfare took them out of the home, they would split them up. At the time, I didn't know I had alternatives because if I had, I would have left and turned myself into welfare. It was so bad that I would have happily lived with any foster family and never returned—end of story.

Growing up, not a day went by that I didn't ask God to kill my mom, and every day, he refused. I got madder and madder. This anger continued to build, to the point where I believe it became an entity of its own. I would have regular migraine headaches and red rages as a child. These periodic appearances were at highly stressed moments in my life. I would just see red and black out. When I came to myself, people said I had done things that I didn't remember. I called it the monster who protected me.

Coming from an Irish background, I feel it is part of our berserk heritage. I have had a spirit of suicidal depression, as well as recognizing that I also have a critical spirit that has kept me safe but no longer serves me, for over thirty years of my adult life. It took Jesus to heal me completely, without the residual lingering or bitterness.

I had to take my mom off the pedestal of my childhood expectations and dreams of a miraculous overnight change. I went from the textbook, classic definition of a narcissistic sadist to a heartbroken, emotionally unhappy prepubescent, stuck in the body of an aging materialist, to a strong, praying, imperfect survivor, a female warrior of Christ, who raised strong warriors for Christ, versus the unrealistic male-driven expectations of a perfect loving mother, like June Cleaver—motherhood personified on the television show *Leave It to Beaver.*

Going over to friends' homes and observing their mothers' parenting skills caused me a lot of internal conflict and conflict about myself and my broken home life. I did not fully understand that my friends were white, economically solvent, with fathers who were prominent and had secure jobs. My mom was a single parent, no high school diploma, raising nine kids by herself. She was never home but always working to keep a roof over our heads and food on the table, doing housework for professionals who could afford a housekeeper. Her parenting skills were lacking, but she was the greatest life coach/teacher and nemesis. She kept me on my knees, praying for her to be killed, healed, or changed for the betterment of our family as a whole.

My family's mentality about our sacred-cow mom was, don't ask, don't tell, and don't dig up that old nasty, dirty stuff we don't want to deal with or know how to handle to heal the hole in our souls. Don't confuse me with the facts because I can't handle the pain; it will kill me. I don't think I can survive to relive the painful parts of my past, so I will stuff it, and maybe it will go away.

This type of generations of traditional dogmas and rules passed down is divisive. Denial is not a river in Egypt. My mom's lack of insight into her impact on the dysfunctionality, demons, and curses attached to our family, generationally, has helped us and hurt us. She is our knowledgeable religious leader and the family matriarch, not subject to criticism, correction, or scrutiny, based on old, strong religiosity that no longer applies or positively impacts the family. Those TV shows of perfect families all over American airwaves and how they were supposed to behave are a form of mind control. It sets America up to fail. My reality and being brainwashed to live up to someone else's expectations was a big lie. But the truth, according to God's Word, is Jesus's love and assurance and clear, strong guidance from the Holy Spirit, for the truth has set me free.

Put on the armor of light. Wear this bright, protective covering. Put aside deeds of darkness.

> You live in a world where darkness is prevalent all around you. You need my light armor to help you see things protecting you from being led astray by the worldliness that surrounds you. I want you to walk in the light with me. Do not despair when you make bad choices that lead you into straying when this happened. Because I am your Savior, I have made provision for all your sins. Moreover, the blood I shed on the cross cleanses you and keeps you walking in the Light. If you confess your sins, I forgive you and cleanse you from all unrighteousness. I am faithful and just, and I delight in your nearest to Me. (Romans 13:12, 14; 1 John 1:7, 9 KJV)

Desperation breeds disobedience and makes us do stupid things, leading to addiction to our flesh. What you feed is what becomes strong (1 Corinthians 15:33). Ricard and Butch, two of my uncles, knew my mom's patterns of discipline and finagled welfare checks on me. They would take me to their bachelor pad and give me drugs to cope with the cluster flock at home. However, one Saturday, they gave me a couple of black beauties and yellow jackets, plus weed to chase the blues away. I went to the bathroom to use the toilet. Then I was floating in the air and saw my body on the toilet floor in a fetal position, with my underwear around my knees.

I was taken out of the bathroom by a huge angel, and it carried me to a white round room and sat me on a wooden stool. All of a sudden, I was watching flashes of movies of me and my life—past, present, and future—in surround sound. The walls were spinning with frame after frame of these movies of my life. I wasn't afraid; I was at peace and no longer felt emotional pain. As I was watching the movies, I noticed that the huge angel had a staff; it was a whitish color.

The angel never said a word; he just watched the movie with me. He was a huge Caucasian male, yet he had androgynous features, male and female, around his face and bone structure and features. He seemed nine feet tall. He had hazel eyes, no wings, and dishwater-blond hair with gold highlights. His hair was parted in the middle and curved underneath his chin in a Little Lord Fauntleroy haircut. He had on red Roman sandals, strapped up to his knees, and wore a white shift that fell to a couple of inches above the knees. Over the shift was a red leather breastplate that covered his torso and attached to a red-leather fringed skirt. Each fringe was about three inches wide and ended in a point. I could see the white shift underneath the leather skirt.

When the movie finished, he looked at me. He never said a word but talked to me mentally. I knew I had to go back and didn't want to. I wanted to stay with the angel, but I knew I couldn't, and he took me back to my body. During the time I was with the angel, I could see the past, present, and future all at once.

While I was observing the movies that were flashing before me on the round wall, the angel and I watched my uncles come into the bathroom and stare at my dead body. No one touched me. They freaked out and ran out of the bathroom while my body lay there on the cold tile floor. Finally, they came in and pulled up my underwear and put me in the bed and talked. Somewhere during that time, I entered my body and woke up. They were very relieved, and they never came for me again.

The second time I died, I was seventeen. My mother moved us back to Kansas City from Washington, in a desperate attempt to reconnect—within her mind—with her soul mate, the man who gave her four love children. Yes, he was a loser of the worst kind and a child molester, just for flavoring. He was one of my siblings' first sexual abusers at the tender age of five or so, in my estimation. At age eleven, he impregnated her. My mom had her doctor friend give her an abortion, and my mom sold all she had, packed up all nine of us, and ran away from him to Washington State when I was about nine or ten.

I knew my mom loved me in her strange way. It's like Jeffrey Dahmer having kids. Before going into the military, I sowed my wild oats. I chose to lose my virginity, got peritonitis, died, was in a two-week coma in the hospital, and missed my graduation in 1977 because I was recuperating. During those two weeks, Jesus showed himself to me, and for those two weeks, we argued as he held and healed me with his shining light that was emanating from his presence. I told him I didn't make a difference. I shouldn't be here; these were not my people, not my real family. Somebody made a mistake and sent me to the wrong place.

Are you sure? Am I supposed to be here because this is hell, and you ain't leaving without me. It was not unlike Jacob, wrestling with the angels (Genesis 35:25–33; Hosea 12:14). I go more into detail in my other book, where I decided to kill myself a third time, and a host of angels with female representatives (angels/witnesses) instructed two tiny cherubim-looking beings to heal my body, plus other things that will blow your mind. It was a glory takeover.

Your Sons and Daughters Will Prophesy

We should encourage children and young people to be open to the Holy Spirit, not only to be baptized in the spirit but to be used by him, but the goal of our instruction is love from a pure heart and a good conscience and sincere faith. First Timothy 1:5 says that from childhood, you have known the sacred writings that can give you the wisdom that leads to salvation through faith, which is in Christ Jesus (Stanley M. Horton).

Kids are nothing but problems—which can be true when the parents lack the necessary skills or don't have a natural affinity to nurture, which is usually passed down from generation to generation.

Culturally speaking, men were supposed to be our protectors, not predators, as I see the worst of them, but not all men are predators. Some good men are silent to the raping and pillaging of our most valuable resources—our youth—lending themselves to the adage, your silence implies your consent. If one does not object to or stand up against something that one does not like or agree with, then one is complicit in permitting it to happen. People like to pretend they are outraged by certain policies, but they do nothing to stop them; their silence gives consent. You know who you are.

As a child, watching television or reading books from my school library, I believed that someday, a white knight in shining armor would come to rescue me from this broken-down palace that I call our world, as I see it. I also realized that, based upon my family's strong matriarchal ties and traditions, I was raised and taught to be more like a man than the stereotypical, weak woman, who needs a man in her life and a relationship so she can feel whole. We females have been taught that we are weak, and we need a man to fix us. Well, hell, I am not broken, and I don't need a man to fix me. So my reality and the real world are at war and have been since I came to this dimension. This is so important for our children to know to take the pressure off both sexes in the future. Did God have children in mind when he inspired the prophet Joel to write, "Your sons and daughters will prophesy" (Joel 2:28)?

Looking at the context, we see the passage begins with the promise, "I will pour out my Spirit on all people (Hebrew, *Kol Basar*, "all flesh"). Then God identifies, first, sons and daughters; then, old men and young men; then, his servants, both men and women (Hebrew, *ha`avadim* and *hashshephachoth*, "the male slaves and the female slaves"). The intent is to show that the promise of the Spirit and the impartation of prophetic gifts is for all people, without regard to race, sex, age, social status, or national origin. These manifestations of prophetic gifts were important from early times, for they were and are evidences of the presence of God among his people (1 Corinthians 14:24–

25, where prophesying will cause visitors to exclaim, "God is really among you!").

The word *prophet* (Hebrew, *Navi'*) comes from an old word meaning "a speaker," but it came to mean "a person who speaks for God, or gods," since there were pagans who claimed to be prophets, such as prophets of Baal (1 Kings 18:19). In most cases, in the Old Testament, those who prophesied (spoke for God) were mature men and women. But God also used children. Samuel is an example.

God used Samuel to speak his word to Eli, when Samuel was still a child. It is true that the Hebrew, by which he is called *hanna'ar* (1 Samuel 3:1), can mean a boy or a young man. However, the Bible says,

> The Lord was with Samuel as he grew up, [emphasis mine] and he let none of his words fall to the ground. And all Israel from Dan to Beersheba recognized that Samuel was attested as a prophet of the Lord. (1 Samuel 3:19–20)

This indicates that he was indeed a young boy when he began to prophesy and that he continued to speak for God "as he grew up." That he "did not yet know the Lord: The word of the Lord had not yet been revealed to him" (1 Samuel 3:7) also shows that he was still a child who had not yet come to know the Lord in a personal way when God first spoke to him.

Another who began to prophesy when he was quite young was Zephaniah. His genealogy in verse 1 of his book shows he was descended from King Hezekiah and that he prophesied in the days of King Josiah. Josiah was eight years old when he became king, and he reigned thirty-one years in Jerusalem. But Zephaniah's genealogy shows there was one more generation between him.

Grandma's Hand

> For this reason I remind you to kindle afresh the gift of God which is in you to the land of my hands. (2 Timothy 1:6)

> For I am mindful of the sincere faith within you, which first well in your grandmother Louise and your mother Eunice, and I am sure that it is in you as well. (2 Timothy 1:5)

> But if any widow has children or grandchildren they must first learn to practice piety with their own family and to make some return to their parents; for this is acceptable in the sight of God. (1 Timothy 5:4)

My grandmother had a vegetable garden in her backyard and would make everyone help with planting. She made us pray to God, Jesus, and Mother Earth after we planted the seeds in her garden, and the vegetables always grew large and tasted oh so good. The neighbors always complimented her on how large and healthy her vegetable gardens were, trying to get her to share her secret. She wouldn't say anything; she'd just smile. They didn't know that she would have all the grandchildren go to her garden and pray over the plants. Need I say more? There's nothing more precious than a child's sincere prayer. God answers your sincere prayers.

My grandmother was an Eastern Star, the female equivalent to the Masons. It was a very mystical, secretive, close-knit female society, almost like a wiccan's coven. And when a member died, my grandmother and her Eastern Star sisters and Mason brethren would have this strange, secret ceremony, in which all of them would sequester themselves alone with the dead body of the deceased member for some time. I overheard one of the Mason's brothers refer to it as "crossing the desert." After that, the dead body of the member would be placed in their home on ice, and the sisters would take turns sitting by the body for three days and nights, wearing their white uniforms and unusual blue star rings, as family and neighbors came by to view the body and pay respect to the deceased. They seem to have an awe, an unusual reverence, and a fear of the Masons and the Eastern Stars.

None of my many aunts or uncles knew anything about the Eastern Stars, but my grandmother always met with these women regularly, until she became a nurse and started drinking heavily, as I got older. When she died, they were there to help her cross the desert.

My grandmother used to say, "It's not the dead you have to be afraid of but the living who can kill you." So I wasn't really scared of ghosts, but I was scared of the movie *Goldfinger*, with Sean Connery playing 007. My uncles used to scare us and tell us that Goldfinger was going to get us at night when we went to bed.

While I was in the military, I was asked to become an Eastern Star by a high-ranking female enlisted person. Even though the female was a good salesperson, who told me about all the benefits of becoming an Eastern Star, I still turned her down. At the time, I didn't know that it was an honor to be asked. All I can remember is my fear of my community members and my grandmother's decline into alcohol and increasingly inferior male partners, who abused and/or sexually molested my uncles and aunts, through the eyes of a child. I had ignorantly connected it to her being an Eastern Star. Knowing what I know now about the Eastern Stars and the high standards of integrity, credibility, and character they espouse, I still would have turned it down because I still don't like rules—except for this: Thou shall not harm and speak my truth, as I understand it.

My grandmother always made healing potions so we wouldn't get sick during the winters, and we never did. She would say cryptic statements, such as that everything a woman needed to abort an unwanted pregnancy was in the kitchen, but she wouldn't tell us what. She had this strange power over people; she could make them do whatever she wanted, especially men. In my life, I've met a few people who could do this, and they usually try to stay out of sight, doing good works in secret or without drawing unnecessary attention to themselves, except for some people who openly use/abuse this gift. As a child of three or four, I remember the bathrooms and water fountains for whites and blacks when my grandmother took me into downtown Kansas City and at a barbeque restaurant, where I first experienced open racism.

Living Angry: My Mama Was a Batterer

One of my few methods of escaping the horrors of my abusive, dysfunctional mother and my noisy, vulnerable, passive/aggressive but lovable seven siblings was to watch television. I never felt safe around my mother; she was raised to believe that kids were seen, not heard. She treated us as objects and slaves to abuse and to relieve her pent-up frustrations on. We had no rights, no opinions, no feelings; we were just beasts of burden. No hugs, no kisses; she carried out punishments that didn't fit the crime and created tension when she was around. She was not protective of her girls. She couldn't keep a man so she forfeited her girls in exchange for the love of a man, any man who paid her the slightest attention. It didn't matter who—married, unmarried, preachers, deacons, ex-convicts, gangsters—you name it; we saw them. I have to give it to her, as she was a tenacious eternal optimist when it came to men.

Every one of them seemed to be "the one," her white knight in shining armor, in her mind. Even though she had nine kids from various other "white nights" (I called them sperm donors), each one was "the one" she thought would take her away, take care of her, cherish her, love her—one she could call her very own. From my perspective, we were all love children. She had an obsessive, ongoing pattern: she'd get pregnant to keep the man; then the man would leave her to sow richer fields. For those nine months while she was pregnant, people treated her with special care, a similar kind of love that she sought from men, until the baby was born.

Some experts in the mental health field would call doing the same thing over and over again and expecting a different outcome a form of insanity. This behavior, in my opinion, got her basic needs met through pregnancy. It was a win/win situation for her.

I was the second oldest, and my older sister and I were forced into being surrogate mothers for our siblings—sixteen hours a day, seven days a week, cooking, baking, cleaning the house, making bottles, cleaning bottles, feeding babies (of which she seem to provide an endless supply), changing shitty diapers, washing clothes, changing clothes, wiping snotty noses, getting the kids to bed, waking them up and getting all of us off to school, making good or else, being a baby bodyguard, siblings protector, educators, and disciplinarians, when she wasn't home, which was all the time. I was next door, at my aunt Mary's home, she and my mom lived in the attached duplex. At the time, my mother had decided to stop working and go on welfare because my older sister, who was eleven, got pregnant by an unknown stranger. My mom suspected her own boyfriend was the father, by whom she had four children. Of course, he was the love of her life, so she was so broken-hearted that she moved all of us from the slums of Kansas City by Greyhound bus to the suburbs of Washington State.

By the time I was twelve, everybody in my immediate and extended family knew that if my head wasn't in a book, I was watching television. It was my great escape and saving grace. I'd tuned out everybody and everything. I was also into Jimi Hendrix's music and liked to wear his kind of clothing. I even cut my hair into an Afro and wore headbands tied around my forehead. After he died, it was rumored that he would slit his forehead and put acid in the cut; therefore, wearing the headband served a multipurpose function, so he could rock out. Headbands became a fashion statement. My favorite article of Jimi Hendrix-type clothing that I possessed was a very thick leather belt with heavy metal studs throughout the belt and a weighty steel buckle.

I was at my aunt Mary's house, watching TV and getting away from my loud, rambunctious siblings. The next thing I knew, my mother suddenly appeared out of nowhere, like a bat out of hell. In her hand was my belt, and she started beating me with the enormously weighty leather belt, with the buckle made of lightweight steel, over my head and any other part she could reach. I screeched and screamed bloody murder with pain as I tried to protect my face and head from the onslaught of her brutal assault. I was distressed, terrified, and confused as to why I was getting this senseless beating. All the while, she was screaming gibberish that I couldn't understand. The next thing I knew, two of my uncles and my aunt pulled her away from me, alarmed and horrified, with bewilderment etched on their faces.

They wouldn't let her go until she had physically calmed down. Angrily, all she said was, "I called you and called you, and you wouldn't answer me. I didn't know where you were!"

One of my youngest aunts calmly and quietly stated, "Lolita, she was here the whole time, watching TV."

She said, "Well, you better answer me when I call you!"

My last butt-whooping was when I was sixteen. I look back on that event like Apache youths who go through their rite of passage when they take part in an ancient test of strength, endurance, and character.

My aunt Frederika came to live with us for a while when her mom died. She and I were the same age. Frederika, my brother Ralphael, my sister Tonet, and I played hooky from school one day, staying at our friend's house next door. Our younger siblings and other little kids in the neighborhood wanted to play hooky with us, but they were too little, and we told them to fuck off. They didn't appreciate it so they went right to our house, knocked on the door, and told my mom we were playing hooky from school next door—talk about being stuck on stupid as teenagers. I made straight A's in school, but intelligence doesn't mean common sense.

My mother was not a happy camper! She marched over next door and yelled from outside, "All of you who belong to me, come out right now!" We were scared shitless. Even my aunt Frederika was shaking in her boots; she had seen my mother in action when it came to her version of butt whippings, which were every weekend, rain or shine. I was scared, but most of all, I was fed up! I was too old to get whippings. I was an A-student in high school. In a month, school would be closed for the summer, so it wasn't like I was going to flunk out of school, I rationalized. I was sick and tired of being sick and tired. At the back of my mind, I knew I had to make my stand here and now. I got mad. I was beside myself, and I felt righteously angry.

I said to myself, "Self, this has to stop." So I decided that when she beat me, I was not going to cry if it was the last thing I did. She was not going to see me cry, so help me God! All the years of physical and mental abuse seemed to have suddenly built up a major storm inside of me. I don't know how I came to this conclusion; it was almost an unconscious decision, not unlike osmosis. It was the same process as when I beat up my abusive big sister, and she left me alone and gave me respect and steered clear of me from then on.

My mom's butt-whipping routine went something like this: you lie down and don't dare get up, nor do you run; if you ran, the beating would be worse, and the extension cord would land wherever it landed (except for the little ones; they were still in training), so you took the butt whooping and hoped to get it over with; that was the unspoken rule in my family, which seems to have been passed down for generations.

We were so conditioned that none of us ever thought of striking back or rebelling against her cruelty. We didn't even know that that was an option; we were so well trained. For me, however, it was the straw that broke the camel's back. I walked in her bedroom to get my whooping, while everyone who had played hooky and those who didn't were crying in their designated order around the corner, awaiting their butt whoopings.

Lolita then yelled so everyone could hear, "Oh no! I ain't whooping no clothes!" When she said that, you could have heard a pin drop! Then, all hell broke loose in the background—the quiet sobbing, whines, moans, whimpers, and sniveling increased in volume and turned into raucous shrieks, wailing, and screams of panic, agony and terror.

After thirteen years of weekend group beatings, I could identify each sibling's sounds of dread, high-pitched bellows, yelling, and gnashing of teeth. The familiar sounds of the various time-honored habitual chanting and crying mantra prayers began in earnest, but with added alarm and passion. Frederika started her long-suffering, low, moaning, muffled sobs, "Ooooh!" My brother Ralphael started crying and pleading for spiritual intervention, saying, "Jesus, help me. I love you, Jesus!" over and over again. My sister Tonet started her mantra of, "My kuchie, my booty, my kuchie, my booty, my kuchie, my booty!"

Mine was, "Uuummm, oohooo!" But not today! I slowly and determinedly took off all my clothes. My mother got an extra-long, thick extension cord and rolled it into itself seven times—in front of us, for the thrill of it. I walked in quietly, looked at the bed, and turned with unwavering hostility. I looked my mother dead in her eyes as I obediently lay down across her bed, buck naked, and she started beating me with the extension cord. As each agonized painful flick flayed my nude body, I didn't cry. I just turned my face toward her and steadily looked her straight in the eyes, as all the hate, fury, resentment, antagonism, and revenge hidden deep inside of me boiled to the surface. I was beyond mad!

All the years of suppressed anger, hurt, frustration, unspeakable pain, guilt, and shame, wishing she was dead, like a volcano ready to blow, I wanted to kill her! All those emotions balled up altogether! I showed it to her with my eyes, and let her have it, with both barrels—feelings I had stuffed for the majority of my sixteen years on this planet, stuck with this female, a monster and slave master, who made us call her mother. After the seventh strike with the extension cord, I determinedly and perversely continued to give her my rock-steady, unyielding stare of seething fury, hate, maddening contempt, and insolence toward her as I glared into her eyes. I barely controlled my undisguised threat of physical violence and revenge. With recognition that something was wrong with this ritual picture—and no sound forthcoming from me—she came out of her sadistic trance.

I saw fleeting expressions of confusion, frustration, hesitation, surprise, shock, awe, and fear. At that precise moment, there appeared to be an undeniable physical, mental, and spiritual shift of power between us. She had a look of utter alarm and recognition that I was at a point of my life where I was thinking the unthinkable, of committing physical harm to her in revenge and payback, the consequence of all the years of the physical, mental, and emotional abuse and torture I had endured from her. Awareness and acknowledgment crossed her face, and for the first time in my life, I knew, without a doubt, that she was scared of me for once.

She said, in a frightened, feeble, cracked voice of caution and uncertainty, "Oh! So you're not going to cry?" It was more of a plea than a statement.

The crying in the background had gotten gradually quiet and still; it was like everyone knew something crucial and momentous had occurred. She immediately recognized that everyone was aware that something significant happened between us. Seemingly to test or validate that this tangible transfer of power had happened, out of desperation, she tried whooping me as hard as she could. This time, she beat me with the extension cord on my back, as I relentlessly, fixedly, and mercilessly continued to look at her, just to let her know that her eyes and her mind were not playing tricks on her.

I was not far off from kicking her ass. Wisdom came to her rescue; she acknowledged that I was using all my self-control not to beat her silly with her cord. The scenario was as old as time itself: this rite of passage of my empowerment I had to take for myself from my mother, the batterer.

Somewhere in the back of my mind, by instinct and out of respect for motherhood and not wanting to embarrass her in front of my siblings, an inner voice told me to leave her with her dignity intact. My acknowledgment from her that I would no longer tolerate her physical and mental abuse was enough. I had made my point, and the relief and sense of freedom I felt was overwhelming. The beating I took stoically hurt so badly that tears involuntarily started running down my face, but no sound came from my lips. I continued to look at her with seething hate and murder. She was only five foot one and weighed 155 pounds. I was nearly five foot five and 185 pounds, a veteran fighter of pure, irreproachable wrath!

After the eleventh lash, I finally made an involuntary muffled cry. She gave me two inferior additional lashes to my back and let me go. She seemed more relieved than I was when I got off the bed and left the room, and she couldn't look me straight in the eye after that day.

At last, I had set a major precedent, not only with my mom but with my siblings, in addition to my adult life as well. I had finally stopped the madness. I was freed! Vengeance is mine, sayeth the Lou. You can only beat a cornered dog so much before it turns on you. When I got old enough, I ran away from home and joined the military, just to get away and rest.

The Adverse Childhood Experiences (ACE) Study—Dr. Vincent Felitti

It was revealed that adverse experiences in childhood were very common, even in white middle-class families, and that these experiences were related to every major chronic illness and social problem with which the United States grapples and spends billions of dollars on.

Mentions of the ACE Study

The CDC's Adverse Childhood Experiences study has shown up in the recent years. It has become a buzz word in social services, public health, education, juvenile justice, mental health, pediatrics, criminal justice, business. Just as everyone should be aware of his or her cholesterol score, so everyone should know her or his ACE score.

The ACE study probably is the most important public health study you've ever heard of. Its origins were in a busy clinic on a quiet street in San Diego. It was 1985, and

Dr. Vincent Felitti was mystified. The physician, chief of Kaiser Permanente, runs a revolutionary department of preventive medicine in San Diego California. He couldn't figure out why each year of the last five years, more than half the people in his obesity program dropped out.

Although people who wanted to shed as few as thirty pounds could participate, the clinic was designed for people who were one hundred to six hundred pounds overweight. Felitti, the doctor who patients trusted implicitly, spoke reverentially. The preventive medicine department he created had become an international beacon for efficient and compassionate care. More than fifty thousand people were screened for diseases that tests and machines could pick up before symptoms appeared. It was the largest medical evaluation site in the world in reducing health care costs, before reducing health care costs was cool.

But the 50 percent dropout rate in the obesity clinic, started in 1980, was driving him crazy. The dropout records astonished him. They had all been losing weight when they left the program, not gaining, that made no sense whatsoever. In his attempt to build a successful program, he was determined to find out why the mystery turned into a twenty-five-year question, involving researchers from the Centers for Disease Control and Prevention and more than seventeen thousand members of the Kaiser Permanente San Diego care program.

In 1985, Dr. Felitti knew that the obesity clinic had a serious problem. He decided to dig deep into the dropouts' medical records. This revealed a couple of surprises: all the dropouts had been born at a normal weight. They didn't gain weight slowly over several years. "I had assumed that people who were 400, 500, 600 pounds would be getting heavier and heavier year after year. In 2,000 people, I did not see it once," says Felitti. When they gained weight, it was abrupt, and then they stabilized. If they lost weight, they regained all of it or more over a very short period.

But this knowledge brought him no closer to solving the mystery. So, he decided to do a face-to-face interview with a couple hundred of the dropouts. He used a standard set of questioning for everyone. Four weeks, nothing unusual came of the inquiries. No clues. The turning point in Felitti's quest came by accident. The physicians were running through yet another series of questions with yet another obesity-program patient: How much did you weigh when you were born? How much did you weigh when you started first grade? How much did you weigh when you entered high school? How old were you when you became sexually active? How old were you when you married?

"I misspoke," he recalls, probably out of discomfort in asking about when she became sexually active. Although physicians are given plenty of training in examining body parts without hesitation, they're given little support in talking about what patients do with some of those body parts. Instead of asking, "How old were you when you were first sexually active," I asked, "How much did you weigh when you were first asked about being sexually active?" The patient, a woman answered, "Forty pounds." He didn't understand what he was hearing. He misspoke the question again. She gave the same answer, burst into tears, and added, "It was when I was four years old, with my father."

He suddenly realized what he had asked. "I remember thinking, 'This is the only the second incest case I've had in 23 years of practice," Felitti recalls. "I didn't know what to do with the information". About 10 days later I ran into the same thing. It was very disturbing. Every other person was providing information about childhood sexual abuse. I thought this can't be true. People would know if that were true. Someone would have told me in medical school. Worried that he was injecting some unconscious bias into the questioning, he asked five of his colleagues to interview the next one hundred patients in the weight program. They turned out the same things, he says. Of the 286 people whom Felitti and his colleagues interviewed, most had been sexually abused as children.

As startling as this was, it turned out to be less significant than another piece of the puzzle that dropped into place during an interview with a woman who had been raped when she was twenty-three years old. In the year after the attack, she told Felitti that she'd gained 105 pounds. "As she was thanking me for asking the question," says Felitti, "she looks down at the carpet and mutters, 'Overweight is overlooked, and that's the way I need to be.'" During that encounter a realization struck Felitti. It's a significant detail that many physicians, psychologists, public health experts, and policymakers haven't yet grasped, nor have they connected the dots.

The obese people that Felitti was interviewing were 100, 200, 300, 400 pounds overweight, but they didn't see their weight as a problem. To them, eating was a fix, a solution. There's a reason an IV drug user calls a dose a fix. One way it was a solution was that it made them feel better. Eating soothed their anxiety, fear, anger, or depression; it worked like alcohol or tobacco or methamphetamines. (Not eating increased their anxiety, depression, and intolerable fear levels).

I attended some of Dr. David Felitti's conferences, and he claims that as a result of the studies, most individuals died by age sixty. By now, you are connecting the dots to our situation and the solutions ordained by God.

Praying for Unsaved Loved Ones

> Oh that man would praise the Lord for his goodness, and his wonderful works to the children of men! For he satisfieth the longing soul, and filleth the hungry soul with goodness. Such as sit in darkness

179

and the shadow of death, being bound in affliction and iron. (Psalm 107:8–10)

When we pray for our unsaved loved ones, let's pray by the power and the blood of Jesus Christ, that God circumcises their hearts and gives them the heart of Jesus. We ask God to put his spirit within them, and let it come through Christ Jesus. Then pray that God opens their hearts to turn to God and to free our loved ones from the slavery of sin. Then we ask God to remove Satan's binding influence upon them and give spiritual sight to them. Ask God to grant them repentance. Lastly, let's pray against them doing the will of Satan and that the Lord will fill them with a supernatural heart, passion, and pursuit of the Lord, our God. This is my declaration in the name of Jesus. In Jesus's name, I pray. Amen (Deuteronomy 36; Ezekiel 11:19, 36–37; John 4:6; Matthew 28–30; Romans 6:17; 2 Timothy 25–26).

Jesus said,

> "Do not be terrified or discouraged, for I am with you wherever you go."
> "Cast your cares on me, and I will sustain you."
> "I am full of grace and truth."

Grace refers to the undeserved favor—love I have for you. Grace is a gift of boundless worth, for it secures your salvation. My love for you is undeserved, unearned, and unfailing, so you can't lose it. Just trust in my unfailing love and rejoice in my salvation (Psalm 55:22; John 1:14; 14:6; Psalm 13:5–6).

People today are barraged by news and messages laced with spin and lies. As a result, cynicism abounds in the world. It's easy for my followers to feel frightened and pessimistic when the mainstream voices in this world speak so heavily against them. Looking at this life through godless, biased lenses will indeed pull you down. Christian courage is the antidote to this poisonous input, and it is nourished by the knowledge that I am always with you. When Elijah was deeply discouraged, he said he was the only one who remained faithful. Yet thousands in Israel had not bowed down to Baal. Elijah was blinded by his isolation in his discouragement.

Challenging circumstances come and go, but I am constantly with you. I am writing the storyline of your life through good times and hard times. I can see the big picture, from before your birth to beyond the grave. I know exactly what you will be like when heaven becomes your forever home, and I am continually working to transform you into this perfect creation. You are royalty in my kingdom (Jesus).

This is based upon the social environment in which I grew up and believed in. It was a collective of unhealthy life experiences, of family members I observed, and I decided that it was not the kind of life I wanted. Hence, my escape into the military. Growing up in Kansas City, Missouri, I was always surrounded by violence in my immediate and extended family. It was how I learned about love—or their kind of love, which was bittersweet. Growing up, no outside intimate relationship in my family lasted more than five years, tops. Growing up, violence and emotional abuse played major roles in every relationship, especially the few that lasted beyond those five years.

I was busy observing and taking note of my relatives' romantic relationships. What I learned as a child was that mostly all the men I grew up around were lower than dogs, so don't expect anything from them. You couldn't trust females because if you had a halfway decent male, some other jealous bitch was going to try to take him away from you, even your sisters. Even back then, we were taught rules for the females in my matriarchal family.

Rule 1: do not have sex or flirt with your siblings' past or current partners/boyfriends/lovers/husbands. That's just being nasty, and as a black female, no one wanted to be called nasty (the same category as a slut and a whore, which was worse than being a prostitute—at least they get paid for services rendered; the above gave it away).

Because of rule 1, unsuspectingly, I was very particular about the type of men I let into my life. I prayed extra hard for several family members, male and female, who actively and unashamedly sexually pursued the men I dumped after dating and had sex with them. (I found this out after

I went into the military.) I am far from perfect, but talk about family teaching you about the real world—it gives it extra-special meaning to sacred familial trust. It didn't exist in my family, but it is totally sacred with God.

I believe that you were listening. I believe that you move at the sound of my voice, so give me doves' eyes. Give me undistracted devotion for only you. I have my eyes on you (Jesus).

Do not be afraid, for I am close beside you, guarding, guiding all the way. Though I am always with you, you are often unaware of my presence. Fear can provide a wake-up call to your heart, alerting you to reconnect with me. And if you knew how much harm I protect you from, you would be astonished! The most important protection I provide is to guard your soul, which is eternal. As my follower, your soul is secure in me. No one can snatch you out of my hand. Moreover, I lead you as you go along your pathway toward heaven. I will be your guide even to the end (Psalm 23:4, John 10:28; 48:14).

The Power of Words of Wisdom

She is my mother, but in a way, having her right there was a constant reminder that she had betrayed us by not protecting us from predators and not telling me the truth about my biological past throughout my entire life. It was hard. I loved her and depended on her, yet I also seethed with resentment, anger, and hurt. Still, something inside me felt like I couldn't trust her, and something deep down in her was broken. After that, I realized that I would not completely trust her the way I always had in my childhood, even though, deep down, I knew she loved me—but it was her kind of love, and I was starved as a result.

As the years flew by, I intuitively knew of a deeper, more fulfilling, lasting kind of love with my higher power, as I understand it.

Eventually, I knew I had to forgive her. She was getting old, and the forgiveness was not for her but for me. And you know what? She needed me more than I needed her, even if I couldn't look at her in the same way. My Creator said I didn't have to hang out with toxic people. It took a while for my siblings to understand that point, as I was healing from years of spiritual, mental, physical, and emotional abuse. In learning to love myself, with the help of angelic beings, with no time limits, grace abounds. I learned about detachment with love—a wonderful life-teaching tool.

Many years later, I was eventually able to go to a family reunion with her and some of my immediate family members. She followed me around like a little puppy dog. It was kind of creepy, especially when all eight of my adult siblings were vying for her attention and were at her beck and call. It brought new meaning to a Bible saying, "I will make your enemy your footstool."

My mother hasn't changed much, but I have. She doesn't use physical abuse anymore; she can't. However, she's a connoisseur in the other areas; she is a master manipulator. At my age, I can sit back and admire her strength, skills, abilities, and talents on my sisters and brothers; she's amazing. My mother was my greatest teacher, and, on a spiritual level, I believe that we are sisters in my soul group, and we agreed for me to have this experience for both of our souls' growth.

When talking about healing herbs, I equate my relationship with my mother with the herb comfrey, a plant that must be beaten in order to squeeze out the beneficial oils.

I Luh Da Lord

If you can dream it, God can make it happen, just as faith the size of a mustard seed can move mountains. Forgiveness is possible, even in seemingly impossible situations.

Do what you can, and leave the rest to me. When you're embroiled in a difficult situation, pour out your heart to me, knowing that I listen and I care. Rely on me, your ever-present help in trouble. Refuse to let your problem become your main focus, no matter how anxious you are to solve it. When you've done all you can for the time being, the best thing to do is simply to wait, finding refreshment in my presence. Don't fall for the lie that you can't enjoy life until the problem has been resolved. In the world, you have trouble, but in me, you may have peace, even amid the mess! Nurture well your thankfulness, for it is the royal road to joy.

Your relationship with me is collaborative—you and me, working together. Look to me for help and guidance, doing whatever you can and trusting me to do what you cannot do. Instead of trying to force things to a premature conclusion, relax and ask me to show you the way you should go—in my timing. Hold my hand in confident trust, beloved, and enjoy the journey in my presence (Psalm 62:8; 46:1; 143:8; 95:2; John 16:33). As my cherished follower, you have received the glorious gift of grace—unearned, undeserved favor. No one and no set of circumstances can strip you of this lavish gift. You belong to me forever, Nothing in all creation will be able to separate you from my love. My presence is with you, for I am the indescribable gift.

Throughout my life and my interactions with my God, as I understand him, I have been told many times that we, as humans, are not the only feeling, sentient beings on this planet and beyond. We are so self-absorbed that we think we are the most important and that everything centers around us, mostly because we don't understand what life is. I was awakened to the fact that everything is energy, including us. And different energies vibrate at different rates, like the blades of a fan, unplugged, without electricity. It looks like it is solid; you can see each blade, and the fan seemingly lacks energy.

However, once you plug the fan into an electrical socket, the fan blades go so fast, full of energy, that you don't see the blades. You could say that the Holy Spirit is the electrical socket and that we are the fan blades that seemingly lack energy. Once the Holy Spirit empowers us, we vibrate at a different frequency, a higher frequency, that people can't see initially, but we know, internally, there has been a change.

We have passed through many of the so-called lesser forms of life, the faster frequency, in our striving toward a higher spiritual form. We have been minerals, dirt, rocks, plants, and animals before incarnating into the human form.

We are curious spirits, and we needed to experience these and learn from them before we were ready to experience lessons in a more complex, denser physical body. I have found that everything is alive, including the planet earth herself. She has feelings, emotions, and needs, just as we have. Right now, she's experiencing pain because of what is being done to her. We are reaching the point of no return, where the damage cannot be reversed. At that point, we will ascend into the new earth because the old one no longer will be capable of handling the stress.

The gospel according to Thomas is a compilation of approximately 114 sayings attributed to Jesus. The opening words of the document read like this: These are the secret words which Jesus, the living one, spoke, and Didymus Judas Thomas wrote down. And he said whosoever finds the interpretation of these signs shall never taste death. Let not him who seeks desist until he finds. When he finds, he will be troubled; when he is troubled, he will marvel, and he will reign over the universe.

The sayings themselves are not the secret. The secret lies in their interpretation. When you find the true answers, it probably will be because it goes against almost everything you've been taught. When the truth of it sets in, you will marvel at it, and then you will know that the power you have is reigning supreme over your life and everything in it. You truly can experience heaven on earth. The gospel of Thomas has been eliminated from the Bible, and there have been many explanations as to the reasoning. Some religious leaders express that if you read it and compare it to what you see in the New Testament, it's a very different kind of book, presenting a quite different Jesus.

When we find writings belonging to Jesus that are not recorded in our primary sources, what is consistent with the ones that we are inclined to believe is that they do indeed come from him. However, when the same seems to be a bit inconsistent with other teachings, we are told they have been edited out due to validity, rather than that they are the sacred truth, intended to be passed into the hands of all people. But these have been reserved for only a few.

Any spotlight on the belief that each person is filled with the same higher power as Jesus, rather than that it is an outside force to be feared, would've changed everything we know about life and our entire history. Just because we are each different does not make us separate. We are all part of the same consciousness, simply taking different forms.

"When you have come to know yourselves, then you will become known, and will realize that it is you who are the sons of the living Father" (Jesus).

I hope you find many, many paths of mysteries from this book and that it gets you started on your path as a truth seeker. There is inexplicable joy in finding out who you are seeking and finding I AM that I AM. I come from a long line of healers. My multicultural background consists of Blackfoot Indians, Irish, and various European and African American ancestry. All my life, I've felt all of my experiences have been for a profound reason, and now all the pieces of the puzzle seem to be coming together. I believe God/Creator and his messengers are nondenominational. Even though I didn't believe in mother Mary, she believed in me. How very humbling. May God, our Father, and the Lord Jesus Christ give you grace and peace with these writings from the Holy Spirit.

I'll rise, and we will rise. I will do it a thousand times a day.

Letter to Mom

Dear Mom,

I just want you to know I do love you and always will. Even though you were not the best mom, I chose you; for that, I am thankful. You were a great teacher. I always watched what you did and sometimes listened to what you said. For that, I thank God. You always told me to pray, no matter what, even though you were never affectionate in my formative years. I did feel your love—or your version of it. Mom, I forgive you for not protecting me and my siblings from the predators of the world when I was growing up, but I need to let you know how it affected me.

They say children learn from what they have to live with.

If children live with criticism, they learn to condemn.

If children live with hostility, they learn to fight.

If children live with pity, they learn to feel sorry for themselves.

If children live with ridicule, they learn to feel shy.

If children live with jealousy, they learn to feel envy.

If children live with shame, they learn to feel guilty.

This is how I was affected, living in your world. I had to leave your world because it was toxic, and it was killing me. I had to find and establish a world of my own and start on my journey to find peace, love, and joy. Your words—"No matter what, always pray"—stayed in my mind. My Creator, higher power, the source, God, goddess of creation, I AM that I AM—whatever name is given—heard my prayers. I need to let you know how it affected me because I became a child again, claiming my birthright with God, who held me in his ever-loving arms.

He taught me this:

If children live with encouragement, they learn confidence.

If children live with tolerance, they learn patience.

If children live with praise, they learn appreciation.

If children live with acceptance, they learn to love.

If children live with approval, they learn to like themselves.

If children live with recognition, they learn it is good to have a goal.

If children live with sharing, they learn generosity.

If children live with honesty, they learn truthfulness.

If children live with fairness, they learn justice.

If children live with kindness and consideration, they learn respect.

If children live with security, they learn to have faith in themselves and those around them.

If children live with friendliness, they learn the world is a nice place to live.

I learned in my journey that I am a child of God. Faith and action on that faith is my divine birthright. As a result, I want to thank you for being a great teacher.

At this time, I am choosing to heal and not be around toxic people or places, for they are triggers for me. I am taking responsibility for my healing and self-care. I love you, and I always will. Thank you again for telling me to always pray.

Love you big,
Lou

For the Lord will judge his people, and he
will repent himself concerning his servants.
(Psalm 135:14)

Jesus said, "Trust me, and don't be afraid."
Do not be frightened by world events or news reports.
These reports are biased, presented as if I do not exist.
News clips show tiny bits of world events from which
the most important factor has been carefully removed:
my presence in the world. Follow the example of David,
who strengthened himself in the Lord when his men were
threatening to stone him. Remember that I Am that I
Am/EL has won the ultimate battle.

As I think about my continuing journey with God, I
look back, as poor black child from very humble beginning,
raised in an active, racially polarized Show Me State.

As I was connecting the dots during my research for
God in this book, another coincidence fell out. The Bible is
a recipe book for everything on earth and some of heaven.

Satan's recipe for me was this:

Add a cup of multigenerational curses and a half cup
of national institutionalized, domestic violence power
and control. Add a dash of historical spiritual abuse and
a pinch of a mountain of attitude: "I am not okay, and the
world is not okay," multiple deaths, and suicide attempts,
which correspond perfectly with Dr. Felitti's ACE study.

To say I was a walking recipe for disaster is an
understatement. Satan is constantly attempting to steal,

kill, and destroy me and you. However, Jesus has plans for me and you. He has shown me, each time rescuing me from the jaws of death, suicide attempts, and black magic.

I cannot begin to adequately describe the indescribable, the glimpses of his awesome glory and power. I am speechless by his unfailing love for me, the inconceivable width, depth, breadth, and length of just his love for me, so I would know, without a doubt, whom I was dealing with, and I know his voice. I don't know, consciously, how, but when he spoke to me, every essence of what I consist of—my soul, my body, my mind, and my spirit—snapped to attention and awakened in the blink of an eye. I knew who was talking to me. I am overcome, and so are you.

I thank Jesus for who he is and that he became the sacrificial lamb for our sins and died for us. I don't know about you, but I didn't have the inclination to do any such thing while I was out in the world. Even now, I lose my bladder, trying to imagine what he went through. Jesus Christ was/is God made in the flesh, Son of God.

Then Jesus gave us the Holy Spirit, the breath of God, to comfort, guide, to teach and reproach. With a healthy mothers love of a new born, reflecting shimmering glimpses, minute portions, that cannot by any means begin to describe the Holy Spirit's unconditional love. This anointing inputs, with in dwelling super powers, glorifying the Almighty Alpha and Omega/God.

Ephesians 4:22-24. Again, not all of God's anointed were Christians.

Rejoice and praise God with me. We are on an adventurous journey, with Jesus holding our hands. Our ultimate destination is heaven. While enjoying the rich relationship he offers us, fear will subside, and joy will rise up within us. We continue to focus on him, thanking and praising him while we wait on his promises. (He answers our prayers with yes, no, or wait.) It is a principle in the Bible; it happens for me, and it'll happen for you.

Jesus says, "Trust me wholeheartedly, beloved for I am your strength and your song" (Isaiah 12:2; Exodus 33:14; 1 Samuel 30:6 NKJV).

Why not pray the simple prayer and begin to experience the greatest blessing of all?

Dear Jesus, I understand that I am a sinner, and yet You loved me enough to die for me. I believe that you are God's Son, my Savior and my Lord.

I call upon You Jesus, to not only bless me with provisions and protection, but you also blessed me with Your promise of eternal life. I surrender my life to You and invite You into every area of my life.

Please forgive me of my sins. Give me a new mind, a new heart, and a new start in life. Direct me in my daily decisions so I can turn from sin and walk in your peace.

Take me to heaven when I die and fill me withYour presence right now. Thank You for hearing my prayer and beginning this relationship with me. I am believing in Your promise that I am saved and I am forgiven. Thank you for this great blessing in Jesus's Name, This my-decree and declaration.

This is some of my story. The Kingdom of Heaven is at Hand!

Printed in the United States
By Bookmasters